Mark His Word

*Cycle B Sermons for Proper 16 through
Christ the King
Based on the Gospel Texts*

Frank Ramirez

CSS Publishing Company, Inc.
Lima, Ohio

MARK HIS WORD
CYCLE B SERMONS FOR PROPER 16 THROUGH CHRIST THE KING
BASED ON GOSPEL TEXTS

FIRST EDITION
Copyright © 2017
by CSS Publishing Co., Inc.

Published by CSS Publishing Company, Inc., Lima, Ohio 45807. All rights reserved. No part of this publication may be reproduced in any manner whatsoever without the prior permission of the publisher, except in the case of brief quotations embodied in critical articles and reviews. Inquiries should be addressed to: CSS Publishing Company, Inc., Permissions Department, 5450 N. Dixie Highway, Lima, Ohio 45807.

Library of Congress Cataloging-in-Publication Data

Names: Ramirez, Frank, 1954- author.
Title: Mark His word : sermons on the Gospel lessons for Proper 16-29, Cycle B / Frank Ramirez.
Description: FIRST EDITION. | Lima, Ohio : CSS Publishing Company, Inc., 2017. | Includes bibliographical references and index. Identifiers: LCCN 2017028523 (print) | LCCN 2017034588 (ebook) | ISBN 9780788029134 (eBook) | ISBN 0788029134 (eBook) | ISBN 9780788029127 (pbk. : alk. paper) | ISBN 0788029126 (pbk. : alk. paper) Subjects: LCSH: Bible. Mark--Sermons. | Common lectionary (1992). Year B. | Church year sermons.
Classification: LCC BS2585.54 (ebook) | LCC BS2585.54 .R36 2017 (print) | DDC 252/.6--dc23
LC record available at https://lccn.loc.gov/2017028523

For more information about CSS Publishing Company resources, visit our website at www.csspub.com, email us at csr@csspub.com, or call (800) 241-4056.

e-book:
ISBN-13: 978-0-7880-2911-0
ISBN-10: 0-7880-2911-8

ISBN-13: 978-0-7880-2913-4
ISBN-10: 0-7880-2913-4   PRINTED IN USA

Contents

No Turning Back

At the dawn of the Space Age it looked like the United States was losing the Space Race — and soundly. The Soviet Union had launched the first artificial satellite in 1957. In response the Vanguard rocket blew up on the pad.

Both nations then began to work on putting a human into space. The American Project Mercury was projected to put a man in orbit by late 1960, but delay after delay — sometimes out of caution and sometimes out of concerns for safety because the rockets continued to blow up, allowed the Soviets to put a man into orbit in April of 1961. The best the Americans could do, a month later, was to send astronaut Alan Shepherd on a fifteen-minute suborbital flight.

Yet on the basis of that suborbital flight, while American morale was low, President John F. Kennedy, at a Joint Session of Congress on May 25, 1961, committed the United States to landing a man on the moon by the end of the decade and bringing him back safely.

Some people questioned the sanity of this proposal. How could we talk about going to the moon when no American had even been into the orbit, and the Soviets seemed to be so far ahead?

Four months later, on September 17, with only one more suborbital flight to America's credit, and the first orbital flight still five months away, Kennedy spoke to an audience at Rice University and explained why this choice was so important. He said:

"We choose to go to the moon. We choose to go to the moon in this decade and do the other things, not because they are easy, but because they are hard, because that goal will serve to organize and measure the best of our energies and skills, because that challenge is one that we are willing to accept, one we are unwilling to postpone, and one which we intend to win, and the others, too."

Did you hear that? The president said that the reason for going was "not because they are easy, but because they are hard."

In today's gospel passage some of the disciples told Jesus that his teachings were too hard. They wanted something easier. And many of them left because, as they said, "This teaching is difficult; who can accept it?" (6:60)

Jesus was not taking the easy road.

Matthew, Luke, and to a lesser extent Mark tell us that Satan offered Jesus an easier road to messiahship. Satan told Jesus he ought to turn stones into bread for his own benefit when he was hungry. He should never have to suffer because surely God would protect him from all harm. And that Jesus, who would be identified in the Revelation of John as the King of kings and Lord of lords, could become king now, and the ruler of all the earthly kingdoms, without having to bear his cross and suffer a humiliating death.

By that time Jesus had already rejected such a temptation, and was taking the much harder path of the suffering servant prophesied in Isaiah. But those who took part in the miraculous feeding of the multitudes weren't looking for a difficult road. They wanted more free bread.

In the gospel of John you either get it or you don't. The first disciples who followed Jesus got it. Nicodemus didn't get it at first. This business about being born again puzzled him and even though he was an expert in Biblical law, he couldn't get away from the literal image of returning to his mother's womb. Later, though, we will see that by the time of Jesus' death, and before his resurrection, he was ready to stand up for Jesus.

The woman at the well got it. She was able to look beyond the literal meaning of "living water," a moving stream that never ends, to the spiritual meaning of the term, and as a result, despite her brokenness, she was able to lead her whole village to a belief in Jesus.

The man born blind got it. The religious experts didn't.

Some people get it. Some don't.

Some people came to Jesus expecting they would no longer have to work to earn their daily bread, that Jesus like Moses could rain manna down from on high. They wanted the bread of life that Jesus offered to be a reprise of the miracle of the loaves and fishes. They had offered the example of the manna as a scriptural way of proving to Jesus that he could only demonstrate his lordship by continuing to provide miraculous bread. Like the bread and circuses offered by the Roman emperors to distract the populace from how bad things really were, they believed Jesus ought to feed them again and again.

However, Jesus replied that their request only proved they were like the people of God in the wilderness who continued to grumble despite God's gracious bounty. Their hardness of heart made them more like Pharaoh than the children of Abraham.

John's gospel used the cinematic technique of seamlessly moving from one locale to another. At first we were with Jesus outdoors, teaching the multitudes. Suddenly, we find that Jesus is speaking to his disciples "in the synagogue at Capernaum (6:59)."

Then Jesus seemed to make things worse. It is not always easy to follow Jesus, especially when he concluded by saying something shocking: "Those who eat my flesh and drink my blood abide in me, and I in them. Just as the living Father sent me, and I live because of the Father, so whoever eats me will live because of me (6:56-57)."

The response of some of his disciples was disheartening: "This teaching is difficult; who can accept it (6:60)?"

These disciples, unlike the Samaritan woman at the well, were unable to get past the literal — and shocking — meaning of this saying. Being born again, having living water to keep one's bucket full, the flesh and blood of Jesus — some people reach the limit of their belief and back away when it gets hard.

John told them that, "It is the spirit that gives life. The flesh is useless. The words that I have spoken to you are spirit and life (6:63)." Jesus told them — and us — that there is a spiritual truth at the heart of these difficult images — and if we are willing to travel the difficult way we will be rewarded.

Then John went on to say: "Because of this many of his disciples turned back and no longer went about with him."

It's one thing for the multitudes to turn away when they don't get what they want. But when disciples, who have traveled with Jesus, heard his words, saw his miracles, turned away, we might ask, should Jesus have simply spoken about the spiritual aspect of this flesh and blood more clearly?

The gospel took place in the real world. Body and blood, broken and spilled, nailed to the cross. It was not always easy. It's not always good to pretend that things are easy, either.

"So Jesus asked the twelve, "Do you also wish to go away?" Simon Peter answered him, "Lord, to whom can we go? You have the words of eternal life. We have come to believe and know that you are the Holy One of God (6:67-69)."

We're so used to the way the other evangelists refer to the twelve apostles we may not notice that in John's gospel this is his first reference to "the twelve." Why is that? Perhaps because until they were tested, until they had this crisis of faith, until other disciples, facing the same difficulty, turned and left, they were not truly the twelve! Just like us

— are we truly the church just because we say we're following Jesus? Sometimes it takes a crisis, a barrier put up by the world, or by other believers, a temptation by Satan, or just proclaiming our belief when others turn away, before we are truly the church.

We can say we believe in Jesus, but being a disciple, being the presence of Jesus in a hurting world, and trusting Jesus, is a lot harder. Yet it is worth doing the things that are hard.

Besides, as Peter says, where else can we go?

Earlier we gave thought to some people referring to the manna in the wilderness, and Jesus reminded them of their hardness of heart. The people in the wilderness, following Moses, had seen many more miracles than any other generation — yet they grumbled, and built a golden calf, and rebelled. They were close to the promised land when Moses sent out twelve spies to scope out the opposition. Two came back saying we can take these guys, and ten came back saying it was impossible.

Joshua, like Peter, stood up against the doubters, and eventually he and the other believing spy, Caleb, entered into the promised land. No one else from that generation lived to see the promise fulfilled.

You may think the world offers you have a lot of choices, but if you do not choose Jesus, where else can you go?

One popular praise chorus, "I Have Decided to Follow Jesus," has the refrain "no turning back, no turning back."

No turning back. According to the story, this song reflects the words of a nineteenth- century Christian from Assam, India. Tortured, and forced to watch his family murdered before his eyes, he proclaimed that he had decided to follow Jesus, and that there was no turning back.

The song continues to reflect his words: "Though no one joins me, still I will follow — no turning back, no turning back."

Finally, before he himself was martyred: "The cross before me, the world behind me — no turning back, no turning back."

According to a Welsh missionary who came to that village, the power of this Christian's witness in the face of suffering and death, led to the eventual conversion of his whole village.

Jesus asks us, his disciples, when things get hard, to go further. Not everyone will. Not everyone wants to. Many are content with civic religion, something that confirms all their prior notions, right and wrong. When things get hard, they turn away.

When told by some of his disciples that his words were hard, Jesus replied, "Then what if you were to see the Son of Man ascending to where he was before (6:62)?" What if we someday see the Son of Man ascending to the Father, in the full sight of the world? When at the name of Jesus every knee at last bows, will we rejoice because we were not turned off by the hard words of Jesus? Will we be the Body of Christ in this world, broken like a loaf of bread so that others may be sustained, witnessing our hardships, to prove that Jesus Christ is Lord? Will the blood of Christ be shed before all through our willingness to give the last measure for our faith?

Or will we be offended by the Body of Christ visible in the homeless, in the refugees of this world, in the witnesses who bravely disdain temptation?

We began this message by reminding you of President Kennedy's resolve that we should attempt difficult things because they are hard. Well, though Kennedy himself was assassinated a little over a year later, and despite the extraordinary difficulties of inventing a whole new technology and doing things that had never been done, despite three deaths on a launch pad that set the program back months while we learned what we had done wrong in our carelessness, Americans succeeded in putting human beings on the moon and bringing them back before the end of the sixties.

Yet in the decades since, how many things have we as a nation backed away from because they were too hard? How often have we as the church taken the easier road?

And how many hard things have we turned away from, as individuals and as a church? How many of us are willing to stand up to the world today? How many will follow faint-hearted folks who call themselves Christians who have taken the easy way? How many will follow the difficult way?

God calls on us to make a choice. Make a good choice. Because at one point or another, there will be no turning back. No turning back.

Amen.

Clean And Unclean

Some think that the purpose of science fiction is to predict the future, but those tend to be people who don't read science fiction. In fact, science fiction is sometimes written to *prevent* the future by holding a mirror to our society to show us truth. Once we get over being startled we realize that we're looking at ourselves.

In 1957, the science fiction writer Isaac Asimov published a short story called *Strikebreaker*. In the story a human society of around thirty thousand individuals lives inside of a small moon. Each job within the society is held by a few families, creating a rigid caste system. The system proves most oppressive to the one family who operates the society's waste disposal system.

The system was totally automated. No individual had any physical contact with human waste. Everything was operated by buttons far away, totally hygenically. But that didn't matter. The family was unclean, and was kept isolated from everyone else in the planetoid because of this prejudice.

Along came an outsider, a sociologist who was studying the society, and when the waste management family went on strike, he operated the machinery, believing that since the society knew how unhappy this family was, they would all work together to remove the barriers.

Instead, the sociologist discovered he himself was now unclean, and must leave the planet as no one would have any contact with him.

As stated earlier, the prejudice doesn't make any rational sense. Like pretty much every job on the planetoid, everything was automated. No one touched anything. But prejudice is not rational. It has nothing to do with reality.

All societies have their own definitions of clean and unclean that sometimes have no real connection with germs or no germs. The biblical rules had nothing to do with scientific knowledge about communicable diseases or microscopic organisms. They provided a mechanism that not only created temporary boundaries but also provided a way for the people to be reconciled with each other.

Clean and unclean, it is true, can exclude people, but as Jesus sought to tell us, these same boundaries allow us to include others. However in his time as well as ours, for some people it is a way of creating permanent boundaries that exclude those we want to define as inferior, or less than worthy of God's grace.

One of the problems is that the society in Jesus' time was centuries removed from the forty years they spent in the desert. In some ways, the time Jesus lived in had as little to do with the people who were freed from slavery in Egypt as our own society. God's people two thousand years ago may have had a temple where they sought to obey the laws set down by Moses, but it was the second temple, not the first, and there were centuries separating those two temples.

Jesus was telling us something very important about the nature of clean and unclean. Exactly what was he trying to say? Since most people are more concerned about what they eat, we might talk about what we're allowed to eat and what we're forbidden to eat, according to the law of Moses.

If you were to ask many people why in the Bible some animals are declared clean, and therefore available to eat, and why some are declared unclean and therefore unavailable to eat, you probably would get some variation of a speech that goes like this: God wanted to protect the people from unclean animals that would give them terrible diseases. This made them a whole lot healthier than their neighbors, because God looked after them.

Now most Christians who love bacon and ham and pork ribs, when asked why we can eat pigs now (and it's usually about pigs, isn't it?) would probably make a face and say that pigs are cleaner now because they're really healthy now. And besides, whether they believe the Ten Commandments should be displayed in public places or not, most Christians would say there's no need to observe the food laws of the Old Testament because we follow the New Testament.

Then there's the odd twist on the healthy choice opinion that comes from the Jewish philosopher Philo of Alexandria, Egypt. Philo lived from 25 BC to 50 AD, and therefore was alive while Jesus was alive. Since he seemed to have thought pork a tasty treat, he also seemed to think that animals like pigs are prohibited, not because they caused disease, but because they tasted so good we lost all sense of control. According to him, "The lawgiver (Moses) forbade all animals of land, sea, or air whose flesh is the finest and fattest, like that of pigs and scaleless fish, knowing that they set a trap for the most slavish of senses, the taste, and that they produced gluttony, an evil dangerous to both soul and body, for gluttony begets indigestion, which is the source of all illnesses and infirmities."

Don't forget that in Genesis, when the world is created, God declares that all the beasts, the creeping things, and the wild animals are good. He doesn't create them and then divide them into different categories. God saw it was all good and he pronounced it all good.

Before the flood, humans and animals were vegetarian. Once Noah emerged from the ark God said, "Every moving thing that lives shall be food for you; and just as I gave you the green plants, I give you everything (Genesis 9:3)."

In Job chapters 39 and 40, God was delighted with all creatures, wild, untamed, domesticated, clean and unclean: including creatures like the crocodile or predatory birds. All of these creatures, according to Psalm 104:27-28, are fed and cared for by God.

So what was the purpose of declaring some animals acceptable for eating and others unacceptable? Although commentators don't always agree with the purpose of temple sacrifice and food laws, many think that the real purpose of this legislation was not to define animals as healthy or unhealthy, but to limit slaughter because all blood belongs to God.

When an animal is slaughtered in the temple, it is killed in the most humane fashion. It's a part of worship. Slaughter becomes a sacred act, and this sacred act is limited to those who are trained to take life. Also, every meal involving meat becomes a sacred feast.

Hunting wild animals was forbidden because they would be slaughtered by an untrained person. Wild animals were consecrated to God for God's purposes, not our own, in the temple system. But if you think about it, hunter/gatherers that depended on wild game, such as many of the Native American tribes, also sanctified those meals by giving thanks to the animal for sharing its life for theirs. And in a similar fashion, some churches in hunting communities have a service of blessing for hunters to remind them of the place we all have on God's great earth.

There weren't just laws for food. The controversy in this scripture begins with an observation by religious busybodies that the disciples of Jesus were eating with "unclean" hands. Now in point of fact they may well have washed their hands, or purified them in an acceptable way.

What they neglected to do was follow the rituals as developed over the centuries by the culture, and these were not culture-wide.

Some Pharisees (not all) were self-appointed guardians of cleanliness. Oddly enough, whoever is in charge of judging clean and unclean tends to consider themselves clean, and the others unclean.

Take something as simple as washing dishes. Some people scrub dishes in soapy water, then dip them again in non-soapy water. Some scrub them in soapy water and rinse them off in running water. Some use a dishwashing machine. Regardless of how we do a task, many of us consider our way the right way, the only way, and everyone else is doing it wrong. They're unclean.

It's kind of like the cruelty of the old children's game of cooties. The idea that there are invisible bugs on someone is ridiculous, but holds tremendous power. Somehow it was the outsider, the weak, the vulnerable, who were most bullied by this game. It was no different with the question of clean and unclean, going beyond scripture, into an elaborate game of heads I win, tails you lose. In this case some Pharisees had ramped up the system on steroids. However Jesus refused to play by the rules of his society, and redefined clean and unclean.

Having been asked, Jesus answered, but not on their terms. He did not admit that he and his disciples were doing anything that was against God's law. Instead, he quoted from the prophet Isaiah to show that these particular Pharisees "abandon the commandment of God and hold to human tradition" (Mark 7:8). As Jesus put it, "Isaiah prophesied rightly about you hypocrites, as it is written, 'This people honors me with their lips, but their hearts are far from me; in vain do they worship me, teaching human precepts as doctrines' (Mark 7:6-7)." Insisting that what truly defiles a person is what comes out of his mouth and not what goes in it, Jesus gave a list of things that make us unclean, and that list did not include a bacon, lettuce, and tomato sandwich.

"It is what comes out of a person that defiles," Jesus said. "For it is from within, from the human heart, that evil intentions come: fornication, theft, murder, adultery, avarice, wickedness, deceit, licentiousness, envy, slander, pride, folly. All these evil things come from within, and they defile a person (Mark 7:21-23)." The implication is that the self-appointed guardians of cleanliness are guilty of some or all of these things themselves. Jesus said as much elsewhere in the gospels. And in the Acts of the Apostles Peter had a vision in which a sheet descended from heaven on which the apostle could see many kinds of animals that he had never eaten. Three times he heard a voice from heaven telling him to eat — and three times he responded that God should know Peter had never polluted his body with unclean animals.

That dream pointed to something deeper — that our own scruples, whatever we may think their source, might cause us to exclude outsiders from becoming insiders in our churches. It wasn't long before Peter learned that God wanted him to transcend the boundaries of clean and unclean as he understood them and travel to visit Cornelius the Centurion, who would have been considered unclean to some of God's people who imagined God did not bless everyone. It wasn't long before Peter realized the Holy Spirit was sending him to baptize Cornelius and his whole household regardless of anyone's ethnic background.

Pushed to its limits, you have separate water fountains and bathrooms for folks with different backgrounds. Some of these restrictions may be enforced with unjust laws. Others may simply be observed by those who consider themselves better than others.

All of us need to establish boundaries, whether we use the rubric of clean or unclean, in order to clarify that our life belongs to God, and porous boundaries that allow for inclusion help us to see more clearly what it means to be part of God's world and not our world.

Take the Amish, for example. Many people seem to think that the Amish are a culture that is frozen in time, that considers technology evil, and that is why their homes are not electrified, and why they drive buggies or ride bicycles.

Keeping in mind that every Amish district is different, according to the dictates of the local bishop, it's important to think about why Amish maintain a distinctive lifestyle.

Since Amish are different in one part of the country from another, we'll talk about the Amish of Elkhart/LaGrange Counties, in Northern Indiana which is the third largest Amish community in the nation. Take computers. You'll find Amish using computers in the public library but not in the home. They'll have computers, electricity, and phones for their businesses, but not in the home. And Amish may hire a driver to take them to work in a factory, but they won't have a car at home.

That's because technology is not evil, and may even be necessary in order for Amish businesses to compete on an equal basis with "English" businesses. (Amish call others English not because of their ethnic background but because of the language they speak).

But the primary question the Amish ask regarding every advance, is whether or not it advances their Christian life. Do technological advances drive families further apart from each other and Christ, or draw them closer? For them clean and unclean is about helpful boundaries, not germs. A computer is not evil. It's a tool. But Amish realize that our obsessions with the computer can draw us farther apart, as well as away from Jesus. How often have you seen people texting each other, even though they're seated side by side? To some, Amish rules seem antiquated and bizarre, and some people react with prejudice against them. It would be better for us to examine our own prejudices, which may be liked the prejudice against the supposedly unclean family in the story *Strikebreaker*. It just shows our prejudices can be so ingrained that we don't even notice them.

When it comes to things like clean and unclean, sometimes what we think is cleaner actually pollutes us. Studies show infants that live around puppies have more immunity. Some societies are having more illnesses because their kids never play in the dirt. Some people use hand sanitizer so much that it has no effect, and in reality leaves them without the natural immunity we should have. Their definition of clean has caused them to be unclean.

As believers it's important to honor the cultures of fellow members, and especially new members. We ought to eat what folks bring to the potluck, even when it's a dish that is very, very strange.

We need not only to accept what other people eat, but learn from newcomers from the church about ways to be closer to Jesus. We should be accepting the wisdom of others, regardless of whether we think they're too old or young. God is working through us all, and we already know that God has made all things good.

In the Christian faith no one is an outsider. Yet slave names abounded on ancient Christian tombs. Slaves were considered inferior, unclean even. According to the historian Eusebius a slave like Onesimus, on whose behalf Paul intervened in his letter to Philemon, became the person in charge of the Ephesian church.

God is with us. God is with us all. God's definition of clean and unclean leaves plenty of wiggle room for us to get together, no matter what barriers society has put up between us. As the gospel says about Jesus, "Thus he declared all foods clean." And thus he declared all people clean as well.

Let us remember that it's what comes out of us that is unclean because it harms others, whenever we say something unthinking, and hurtful, and untrue.

Amen.

(You can find the story "Strikebreaker" most easily in the anthology "Nightfall and Other Stories," by Isaac Asimov. The quotation from Philo is from "Purity and Danger" by Mary Douglass, pp 45-46. With regards to matters of clean and unclean, some of the concepts from the present author's reading are to be found in the study book he co-authored with Robert W. Neff titled "Ten Reasons To Love Leviticus," published in 2016 by Brethren Press.)

Call It Like You See It

In Tobit, one of the books of the Apocrypha, the hero To-bias sets out on a journey to call in a loan owed to his father, who has gone blind. He will return with a bride and a cure for his father's blindness. But he sets out on the journey with a young man — who he does not recognize as an angel — and a faithful dog.

Well, sort of. There are several versions of this apocryphal book. In the version that was current among Greek-speaking Jews, there is a dog. In the versions that circulated among Jews closer to Jerusalem, there is no dog. That's because in many of the nations in ancient times, as well as Jews who had become acculturated to the Greek speaking world, dogs were acceptable as pets and companions.

It's hard to say just when dogs and humans became boon companions. Archaeologists who examine the campfires of human settlements notice that around ten thousand years ago dogs found a place around the fire. Some of the bones of the animals found in ancient trash heaps have bite marks that fit the mouth of a dog, not a human.

So at some point dogs and humans began to share their lives together. It's not clear if humans invited the dogs into their homes, or if some dogs invited themselves, providing protection and help with hunting. But it's thought that those dogs that were less feral and found a way to work with peo-ple ate better and were more successful than wild dogs, and so the genes for domesticity were passed on. And the partnership has been good both ways. Studies show, for instance, that infants that grow up around dogs have more immunities. And there's nothing like the loyalty of a dog when it comes to protection.

When people became less nomadic and began to live in one place, with domesticated cattle, sheep, and other creatures, dogs still worked, but for some people they became more like pets. Then again some cultures had no use for them.

But in the Palestinian region, including Galilee and Jerusalem, dogs were scavengers, diseased ridden animals that were despised by the local population. And that continued through the time of Jesus. So when Jesus, in today's story, compared the children of a Gentile woman to dogs, it was *not* a compliment.

Today's gospel passage can make us cringe. It comes after we see Jesus at his best, and then it seems to show Jesus at his worst, echoing the prejudices of his contemporaries, comparing outsiders to a scavenging animals.

The passage follows the question of clean and unclean. Jesus had stated we're made unclean not by what is outside of us, but what comes from within.

Now every culture has its own "cooties," a code of cleanliness that has little to do with actually killing germs. But by drawing boundaries, outsiders give insiders the heebie jeebies, and the outsiders have their own boundaries about whether they'll eat horses, cheese, corn, dogs, or corn dogs. It doesn't have to make sense, but it's very real to the culture.

Now in the verses that precede this story Jesus redefined clean and unclean. It wasn't what rituals people observed, Jesus taught, that made you clean or unclean, it's what we say and do. It's not what goes in our mouths, but what comes out of our mouths.

So it's ironic that having talked about how definitions of insiders and outsiders have been changed under the new covenant, Jesus seems to get put to the clean/unclean test. And at first he doesn't come out looking so good.

Having traveled to the Gentile region of Tyre, Jesus encounters a Syro-Phoenician woman whose daughter is very, very ill. The woman pleads for Jesus to heal her.

What we'd like to see is a repeat of what happens in John's gospel, where Jesus asks the Samaritan woman at the well to drink out of her drinking cup. No, no, no, no, no, Jesus wasn't supposed to talk to a woman. Jesus wasn't supposed to talk to a Samaritan woman. Jesus wasn't supposed to drink out of the same cup as a Samaritan. He definitely wasn't supposed to share a cup with a Samaritan woman, especially one who has been married five times before and is now living with her current beaux. But Jesus ignores all these boundaries with the result that a whole Samaritan village comes to believe in the Lord.

And when hypocrites criticize him for a letting a woman throw herself at his feet, wipe his feet with her hair and her tears, breaking clean/unclean boundaries left and right, Jesus scolds his critics for not recognizing what this woman has done.

Also, earlier in this gospel Jesus had cured the daughter of the president of the synagogue. Shouldn't he do the same for the daughter of the Syro-Phoenician woman?

Instead, he replies to her urgent request, "Let the children be fed first, for it is not fair to take the children's food and throw it to the dogs (7:27)." He compares the Gentile daughter to a dog.

One wonders, perhaps, if Jesus, fully human and fully divine, was simply exhausted. It's kind of like those commercials where nice people become rude and abusive, no longer looking like themselves but transformed into a celebrity with a reputation for behaving badly — at least until someone offers them a candy bar, saying, "You're not yourself when you're hungry." The person then returns to normal. Do you think Jesus temporarily had low blood sugar?

He had, after all, been seeking a place where he could pray by himself when the demands of ministry called him into action. Maybe he thought he would be unrecognized in Gentile territory.

The ancient church fathers wanted to, like the hymn, "Stand up, stand up for Jesus," making excuses for his seeming bad behavior.

Maybe that's why Ambrose said, "If God invariably listened to every supplicant equally, he might appear to us to act from some necessity rather than from his own free will." (*Concerning the Mysteries*, 1.3) In other words, Jesus can't grant everyone their prayer because it would like he *had* to do something, rather than *chose* to do something.

Augustine goes so far as to tell us *not* to do what Jesus said, when he wrote: "Some people, intent on severe disciplinary precepts, admonish us to rebuke the restless and not to give what is holy to dogs, to consider a despiser of the church as a heathen, to cut off from the unified structure of the body the member who causes scandal. These may so disturb the peace of the church that they try prematurely to separate out the wheat from the chaff before the proper time, and blinded by this pretext they themselves become separated from the unity of Christ." (Faith and Works 4.6)

The good thing is that the Syro-Phoenician woman did not slink away. She challenged Jesus with regards to his society's notions of clean and unclean. Her response was gentle, even funny, but to the point. "Sir, even the dogs under the table eat the children's crumbs (7:28)."

I like the way the Common English Bible opens his reply: "Good answer!" Jesus responds by immediately healing her daughter.

Whether Jesus meant his first response as an object lesson for his disciples — and for us! — the fact remains that when the Syro-Phoenician woman called him on it, he did not stick with a position that sounds racist.

God invites tough dialogue. Abraham argued with God over the number of righteous people who, if found in Sodom and Gomorrah, would save the cities of the plain. Moses talks God out of a resolution to destroy the chosen people in the desert and start all over with Moses' descendants. Job rails against all that has occurred to him and complains that he cannot get a fair hearing before God about his laments! The prophet Habakkuk takes God to task not once, but twice, for the unpunished injustice in his society. Jonah argued with God. The woman at the well didn't back down from challenging Jesus. The psalms and the book of Lamentations call into question God's actions or inaction.

When we talk back to God we show we take God personally, as we should a personal God.

Far from being satisfied with things as they were, the evangelist Mark seemed to encourage his readers to question situations of injustice. Again and again outsiders recognize Jesus' healing presence while his own people miss the point entirely. It's a consistent theme in Mark and the other gospels. Insiders don't get it. Outsiders recognize Jesus for who he is.

The Syro-Phoenician woman called it like she saw it — even though it was Jesus she confronted. Daring — yet she was not condemned. What does this mean for us?

We sometimes find ourselves in the uncomfortable position of hearing people in power, and people who we thought we knew well, say outrageous things about other people. They may repeat racist jokes. They may repeat racial stereotypes. They may condemn an entire people, or religion, or nation.

We are also to call things as we see them. Confront racism, ignorance, and prejudice in the church. Avoid making excuses. And examine as well what we are saying or doing to perpetuate racial stereotypes or misinformation.

Most of us don't like confrontation. We'd rather just let it go. But we can't.

The Syro-Phoenician woman didn't respond by spouting hatred at Jesus. She made that clever remark about dog, tables, and children. We too can open a dialogue that is less condemnatory and more conciliatory. Revelation 7:9 gives us a picture of "…a great multitude that no one could count, from every nation, from all tribes and peoples and languages, standing before the throne and before the Lamb…." Jesus challenges us to be better than we are, and to challenge each other to do the same.

Call it like you see it. Respond - respond gently at first if you have to, but firmly.

Today's passage continues with another story of healing, this one involving the ministry of touch. Jesus took the long way to Galilee and the Decapolis, traveling from Sidon through Tyre which is 22 miles north, and the opposite direction from where he ended up. There he met a deaf man who is brought by his friends to Jesus.

Illness in biblical times meant quarantine from loved ones and from the circles of support that most of us take for granted. These friends were ignoring the custom of the time of isolating the sick by taking his part and bringing him before the great healer.

The scriptures say, "Then looking up to heaven, he sighed and said to him, "Ephphatha," that is, "Be opened." (7:34). The word for sigh makes it clear that Jesus shared the suffering, for he expressed deep distress.

Mark focused on the physical description of what happened, outlining how Jesus made the healing poultice. This is a story about touching the sick, touching without fear.

One sees that in both stories words change perception — the daughter of a Gentile, and a person who was unable to hear, both of them in their own way untouchable, are not only healed, they are included. Those who were present and witnessed, and we who watch from the distance of two thousand years, are transformed.

As the church we are to minister to outsiders, to the untouchable. Being the church is more than ministering to ourselves, caring that the budget is met, and supporting those within the church. These are important things, but the real ministering for Jesus is outside our doors and our comfort zone.

At the beginning of this sequence of events, Jesus attempted to retreat from the world but active ministry brought him back into the midst of the suffering. Rest assured he will again set aside time to be alone in prayer, but when we are called into the fray, we must go forward in faith that we will be equipped by God to do great things.

This is an uncomfortable passage, but sometimes we need to be pushed out of our comfort zone and into the ministry of Jesus. We can always hope it doesn't happen too often, but we can also pray that in God's time and with God's encouragement, we will be pushed to be better than we think we are, and to do greater things than we have done before, to the glory of God and our neighbor's good.

Amen.

The Secret Man

In 1972 two relatively unknown reporters, Bob Woodward and Carl Bernstein of the Washington Post, began to cover what was described by one person as "a third rate burglary."

On June 17, 1972, five men were arrested for breaking into the Watergate Hotel, where the Democratic National Committee had its headquarters. They were attempting to place a wiretap in the party offices. Even though it was an election year, the story didn't seem to have much traction, because President Richard Nixon had such a large lead over anyone who might oppose him.

Yet with diligence, hard work, and some luck Woodward and Bernstein discovered that what seemed to be a vague connection with the Committee to Reelect the President, had turned into a breathtaking story of political intrigue, corruption, and obstruction of justice. Two books, *All The President's Men*, and *The Final Days*, resulted from their reporting, as well as the movie *All the President's Men*. Ultimately, a president was forced to resign.

It became apparent in their reporting that one of the two reporters had an inside source that came to be named after the title of an infamous pornographic film, not because Woodward or Bernstein chose that name, but because someone else at the Post thought it sounded exciting.

Bob Woodward tended to refer to this mysterious source as MF, which stood for "my friend." Many people assumed it had to be someone who was part of the Nixon White House, but as it turned out, MF also stands for "Mark Felt," who at the time of the Watergate burglary was the number two man at the FBI. Felt resented the fact that civil servants had been installed as directors of the FBI after the death of its founder, J. Edgar Hoover. He resented the attitude of many in the Nixon White House that they were above the law, and could control any investigation by the FBI. Felt did not so much reveal information about the criminal acts he'd discovered as he invited Woodward to tell him what the two reporters were discovering, so he could confirm or deny their work.

For decades after the Watergate scandal it was a favorite parlor game for amateur and professional sleuths to name the source. Woodward never responded aye or nay, because he was committed to keeping his source's identity secret until either that source gave him permission, which didn't seem likely, or else died. That was the agreement, and Woodward meant to keep it.

Then, decades later, Woodward realized his source, who zealously hid his identity, had begun to sink into a cordial dementia. Even though he didn't seem to be able to give informed consent, he told his family that he was the deep source. The family allowed him to make that announcement to reporters, and to be featured on the cover of a major magazine even though that source was unable to answer any questions about what he had done, nor could he even remember the people involved in the Watergate Scandal.

Reluctantly Woodward decided to publish a book called *The Secret Man*.

Mark Felt was "The Secret Man," who denied on several occasions that he was that secret source behind Woodward and Bernstein. Felt had planned for his identity to be revealed only after his death, but his dementia took events out of his control.

In the gospel of Mark it was Jesus who sought to be "The Secret Man." Jesus told people to keep his actions and his words secret — although it didn't do much good. In the first half of the gospel of Mark, Jesus didn't want his disciples or others to tell the world about him. They did anyways.

The gospel of Matthew concludes with these instructions by the Savior to his apostles: "Go therefore and make disciples of all nations, baptizing them in the name of the Father and of the Son and of the Holy Spirit, and teaching them to obey everything that I have commanded you (Matthew 28:19-20).

But in Mark, again and again, he insisted that his work must remain secret, The questions arise: Why wouldn't Jesus let people talk about what he was doing? Was Jesus hiding something? Why didn't he want people to tell his story?

Actually, this secrecy has a name. Some refer to it as the Messianic Secret. It has been the subject of many books and articles. I'm going to suggest that the reason Jesus did not want people to talk about him and his ministry was because that information was incomplete.

That's because as important as his work was as a teacher, healer, wonder worker, leader, story teller, and Messiah was, any knowledge received through these events is incomplete.

That's because you only know Jesus through the cross. If you don't include the cross in your calculations, you don't know Jesus.

Is Jesus a teacher? Yes he is!

Is Jesus a healer? Yes he is!

Is Jesus a wonder worker? Yes he is!

Is Jesus a story teller? Yes he is!

Is Jesus a leader? Yes he is!

Is Jesus a story teller? Yes he is!

Is Jesus the Christ, the Messiah, the Savior of the world? Yes he is!

Consider the first eight chapters of Mark.

In the very first chapter a demon correctly identifies Jesus of Nazareth as "the Holy One of God (1:24)." Jesus silences the demon, because while Jesus is the Holy One of God, that's not all he is, and there is no mention of the cross.

Only a few verses later Jesus was again exorcising demons from the ill, and Jesus was commanding them to silence.

The first chapter concludes with Jesus healing a leper, and insisting "...that you say nothing to anyone... (1:44). The leper disobeys Jesus. One can hardly blame him for spreading the news, but this is not news that Jesus wishes to be spread.

Jesus continued his healing and teaching ministry. At one point Jesus told those who were healed "...not to make him known (3:12)."

Jesus stilled the storm, and yet when he spoke in parables he didn't explain what they meant. Mark's gospel says that Jesus, "did not speak to them except in parables, but he explained everything in private to his disciples (4:34)."

The fifth chapter is even more puzzling. Jesus healed a man who was a danger to himself, his family, and the villagers, inhabited as he was by Legion, because there were so many demons within him. When the man was healed he desired to follow Jesus, but Jesus refused to allow this saying instead, "Go home to your friends, and tell them how much the Lord has done for you, and what mercy he has shown you (5:19)." This limited the number of people he could tell about what Jesus shared with him to a small circle.

And later in that same chapter, after raising the daughter of Jairus, the synagogue official, Jesus "...strictly ordered them that no one should know this..." (5:43).

The ministry of the good news about the kingdom continued to build. Multitudes were fed, the sick were healed, and the disciples were sent out on their own missionary trip to drive out demons. It seemed as if the picture was being filled in about who Jesus was.

As the seventh chapter concludes, Jesus healed a deaf person and "...ordered them to tell no one; but the more he ordered them, the more zealously they proclaimed it (7:36).

Should we be surprised? Some have wondered — are we really seeing a bit of reverse psychology? Tell someone to keep something secret, and they'll blab it everywhere.

The Pharisees confronted Jesus in the eighth chapter and demanded a sign. Here we see that if you are known as a wonder worker, people will want you to work wonders, and nothing more. Perhaps something about the reason for the Messianic Secret is revealed when Jesus, with a deep and heartfelt sigh, said, "Why does this generation ask for a sign? Truly I tell you, no sign will be given to this generation (8:12)."

Once again Jesus fed the multitudes. Afterward, he healed a man who was blind, and Jesus tried to keep this action secret, for as it says in Mark 8:26, "Then he sent him away to his home, saying, 'Do not even go into the village.'"

Then we get to what matters, when The Secret Man was finally ready to let the cat out of the bag. Jesus asked the disciples what people were saying about him. How were they identifying him? At first they hemmed and hawed, perhaps worried that they would get the wrong answer — Jesus was John the Baptist, or Elijah, or one of the prophets come back from the dead.

But Peter gave the correct answer — Jesus was the Messiah.

What does that mean? In that day there were many different brands of Judaism, just as we have many different denominations today. Some of these groups believed in a Messiah. Some didn't. And they understood what the Messiah might be in different ways.

There were Pharisees who, despite the legalism displayed by those who challenged Jesus, tended to be the ones who served the ordinary people the most often as leaders in the synagogues.

There were the Saducees, who tended to be richer, well placed politically or religiously, who did not believe in an afterlife and didn't need a Messiah, because they believed when God made someone rich it was because God favored them over the poor. Why would they want things to change?

There was the Dead Sea Community, sometimes called the Essenes, who had their own holy books on top of the others recognized by their co-religionists, who lived peacefully, though they planned to take up arms once the Holy War broke out to drive out the Romans and restore God's kingdom through the sword. Their Messiah would not come until those end times!

There were the guerrilla fighters, known as Zealots or Sicarii, who had no intention of waiting for God to bring the kingdom into the world. They were going to do it themselves or die trying.

That's why, even when Peter got the right answer, asserting that Jesus was the Messiah, he had the wrong understanding of what the Messiah would do. So Jesus "sternly ordered them not to tell anyone about him" (8:30). Not yet. Not until "he began to teach them that the Son of Man must undergo great suffering, and be rejected by the elders, the chief priests, and the scribes, and be killed, and after three days rise again" (8:31). This is what the disciples needed to know. This is what we need to know. After this, there is no reason for the Messianic Secret, because Jesus will be turning his eyes toward Jerusalem. Before the world all will see that he will undergo great suffering, rejection, torment, and death. All will see that he will rise from the dead."

And not only Jesus. Make no mistake. Jesus told not only his disciples, but the crowd, "If any want to become my followers, let them deny themselves and take up their cross and follow me. For those who want to save their life will lose it, and those who lose their life for my sake, and for the sake of the gospel, will save it (8:34-35)."

This is crucial. What does it mean for us to take up our cross and follow Jesus? For many people it means that we must accept the suffering that is the lot of every human being. We hurt in different ways, physically, emotionally, and spiritually. Some of us suffer from diabetes, arthritis, or cardiac conditions. Some of us suffer emotionally. For some of us what comes easy to others proves next to impossible. There is so much suffering to which Jesus came to minister, and which we are called to minister to as well.

I think the crucial thing about the cross is that Jesus did not deserve it. Jesus was not guilty of a crime. Jesus was not exposed to public humiliation and a complete loss of face. Jesus was covered with shame for something he had not done, but he accepted it.

Certainly we don't deserve the physical and emotional suffering we experience either. But I wonder if we only truly pick up our cross and follow Jesus when we stand up for him, stand up for the gospel, and receive shame, false accusations, loss of face, for his name, for the sake of the good news?

When we stand up for refugees, for outsiders, for those who are reviled by the public, and share their shame, we are picking up our cross and following Jesus. When we risk becoming unpopular, losing our friends, and even face arrest, like those who marched for Civil Rights, keeping their faith before them and their Bibles in their hands, then we are picking up our cross and following Jesus.

When we serve the sick and suffering who are reviled by the world, we are picking up our cross and following Jesus.

When we do so, our reward is great. Jesus concluded this chapter by saying that if we prefer the world's regard, "… what will it profit them to gain the whole world and forfeit their life? Indeed, what can they give in return for their life? Those who are ashamed of me and of my words in this adulterous and sinful generation, of them the Son of Man will also be ashamed when he comes in the glory of his Father with the holy angels (8:36-38).

Finally, in the ninth chapter, we see glory. We see why Jesus accepts the cross and why we do too. Jesus takes three apostles up a high mountain and he is transfigured, transformed, visible as a creature of light, in the presence of Moses and Elijah, and we know him. And while Jesus was the source of the light, we will be revealed as reflecting the light, sharing God's glory, our crosses transfigured and transformed as well.

Once again:

Is Jesus a teacher? Yes he is!

Is Jesus a healer? Yes he is!

Is Jesus a wonder worker? Yes he is!

Is Jesus a leader? Yes he is!

Is Jesus the Christ, the Messiah, the Savior of the world? Yes he is!

Was Jesus going to travel to Jerusalem and be brutalized by the political and religious leaders of the city, betrayed, turned over to Roman authorities, and be crucified? Yes he was.

Remember, even though Peter got the secret identity right, he still got it wrong because he wanted Jesus to become the Christ without the cross.

Many of us want our Christianity without the cross. We are not willing to share both suffering and glory. We do not wish to risk the world's disdain. Let's stand by Jesus. Let's stand by the cross. Let's carry our own cross. Let's carry out own cross — all the way. All the way to glory.

The secret is out anyway.

Amen.

Winner And Still Champion

I know we're talking about a text from the gospel of Mark, but forgive me if I begin by quoting from the Acts of the Apostles because it makes a point about childhood in that era. In Acts 22:3, the apostle Paul begins to make his defense before a hostile crowd of his countrymen. He had been falsely accused of bringing a Gentile into the inner court of the temple in Jerusalem, and it was his intention to show that he had been diligent in his practice of the faith his whole life.

So he began: "I am a Jew, born in Tarsus in Cilicia, but brought up in this city at the feet of Gamaliel, educated strictly according to our ancestral law, being zealous for God, just as all of you are today."

His point was that he had a foot in two worlds. Because he was born in Tarsus he was part of the dispersion of the Jews throughout the Roman Empire. However, because his parents wanted to make sure he was taught correctly, the family moved to Jerusalem, where he could study under the great Jewish teacher Gamalial, This turned him into a Jerusalem Jew.

What is not obvious in this statement is that according to the customs of his day Paul would have begun the serious study of the Hebrew Bible at the age of 5. And this would be serious study, because although Paul may have known Greek and Aramaic, Hebrew was a church language that would have required serious study.

At the age of five! But childhood was something different in Paul's day. We think of children as cute, wonderful, darling little things. In the first-century world children were closer to the bottom rung of the food chain. They were only valued as they became useful, working in the family business, on the farm, or taking up serious studies that would determine the future course of their lives.

This is important, because in this passage, where Jesus used a child as an example of how to receive Jesus, the comparison he was trying to make was much different than we would make.

This passage begins with Jesus, continuing to teach about his coming death and resurrection. The scripture tells us that in the wake of the Transfiguration, Jesus and his disciples returned to Galilee, in part to avoid his movements being tracked.

Jesus said, very clearly, "The Son of Man is to be betrayed into human hands, and they will kill him, and three days after being killed, he will rise again" (9:31).

Jesus described this way to the cross with words reminiscent of Daniel 7 and Isaiah 53. These were two very important scriptures from the Hebrew Bible for understanding what it meant for Jesus to be the Messiah.

Daniel 7:13-14 presented a clear picture of the glory of this messiah who descended to the earth. The prophet records a dreamlike sequence —

> *As I watched in the night visions, I saw one like a human being coming with the clouds of heaven. And he came to the Ancient One and was presented before him. To him was given dominion and glory and kingship; that all peoples, nations, and languages should serve him. His dominion is an everlasting dominion that shall not pass away, and his kingship is one that shall never be destroyed.*

But the prophet wanted to make it clear that the powers of darkness still reigned, and would vent his anger against God's holy ones. This unholy monster would:

> ...*speak words against the most high, shall wear out the holy ones of the most high, and shall attempt to change the sacred seasons and the law; and they shall be given into his power for a time, two times, and half a time (Daniel 7:25).*

The phrase about a time, two, times and half a time equates to the number 3 1/2, half of the perfect number seven. This meant that darkness would reign imperfectly for a limited time before God would intervene. Who would suffer? According to Isaiah it was the suffering servant of the Lord. Believers of that time were counting on one like a Son of Man, as described in Daniel, but many believed that this Son of Man would suffer for their sins. This would be both terrible and wonderful to see:

> *Surely he has borne our infirmities and carried our diseases; yet we accounted him stricken, struck down by God, and afflicted. But he was wounded for our transgressions, crushed for our iniquities; upon him was the punishment that made us whole, and by his bruises we are healed. All we like sheep have gone astray; we have all turned to our own way, and the LORD has laid on him the iniquity of us all. He was oppressed, and he was afflicted, yet he did not open his mouth; like a lamb that is led to the slaughter, and like a sheep that before its shearers is silent, so he did not open his mouth (Isaiah 53:4-7).*

Surely these were among the scriptures Jesus taught his disciples. He was attempting to show them that his death and resurrection were described in scripture. Still as Mark wrote, "But they did not understand what he was saying and were afraid to ask him (9:30).

Possibly they were intimidated but if we are afraid to ask questions we are missing out on the opportunity to grow in faith. Not only that, failure to ask questions may lead to accepting a false and even damnable doctrine.

In his autobiography the writer Mark Twain pointed out that his mother, who was a faithful church goer in a slave state before the Civil War, never heard a word against slavery from the pulpit. No one questioned its morality. It was taken for granted that God ordained slavery.

It's important to distinguish between slavery in the Roman Empire and American slavery. Both are wrong, but in the ancient world people might be born into slavery, be captured in war and made a slave, or chose slavery in order to settle debts. But slaves were not considered inferior because of their race. Anyone could be a slave, and slaves could work themselves out of slavery.

American slavery was based on the false belief that some people were inferior to others, and were therefore meant to be slaves. That is a whole other sin.

Jesus could have been preaching a spell binder as they traveled to Capernaum, but the disciples never heard a word of it. They were too busy arguing. Once they arrived at Capernaum, and were, perhaps, resting in the home of Simon and Andrew, where earlier in the gospel Jesus healed Simon Peter's mother-in-law, Jesus asked what they had been talking about on the road.

They were silent — embarrassed — wrong.

If they were reluctant to ask questions, they were even less willing to talk about their argument, because they'd been talking about which one of them was the greatest.

This leads to a radical lesson about status. Rank and priority were crucial questions in the Roman Empire. People were very protective about their status. They remembered every slight and they never forgot, no matter how high a person rose, where they began.

Mark wrote: "He sat down, called the twelve, and said to them, "Whoever wants to be first must be last of all and servant of all (9:35).

Although Mark rarely pictured Jesus as sitting to teach, that was the standard way for a teacher to teach. The disciples would also teach. Sitting down in this instance was important because, "Then he took a little child and put it among them; and taking it in his arms, he said to them, "Whoever welcomes one such child in my name welcomes me, and whoever welcomes me welcomes not me but the one who sent me (9:36-37).

What Jesus was doing was acting out a parable. Perhaps this child was part of the Simon and Andrew's household. The text uses the Greek word *agkale* that refers to a bent arm. Jesus took the child in his arms and embraced him.

This child might have been trying to behave and stay out of the way of the important grownups. Suddenly he found himself at the center of attention. This child, at the bottom of the food chain, was raised to the status of the Son of Man, who sits in glory on a cloud.

The disciples were worried about their place in the kingdom and they were asking the wrong question. In order to stand with the Son of Man, the suffering servant who would bear the sins of all for the glory of God's kingdom, it was necessary to lose status, not gain it.

In Paul's letter to the Philippians he told them — and us — that Jesus was obedient to God by taking on the form of a slave and dying on the cross. We see Jesus taking on the form of a slave when he shocks his apostles by washing their feet. Only a slave would do that. To be faithful is to become a slave.

Felix, the governor of Judea from 52-59 AD, was described with disdain by the Roman historian Tacitias, his pen dripping with venom because Felix was a freedman. The feeling was that born a slave, always a slave, and that sometimes even a freedman could not escape that taint.

Christians didn't seem to believe that way. There is evidence Priscilla and Aquila, wife and husband, who appear in the Acts of the Apostles, were a noble woman and a freedman. His status as a former slave did not keep him from being a companion of Paul and a teacher of the good news with his wife.

Around the year 115 AD Pliny the Younger, governor of Bithinia, who wrote a letter to Emperor Trajan asking what to do about the illegal Christian faith, described his methodology to discover what it was the Christians were doing. To get information he tortured two female slaves who were also deacons in the church. What he discovered was that these Christians were meeting before dawn to share a meal, sing hymns, and pray to Christ as to a God. This tells us that slaves and women, two classes of humans who were considered inferior, were considered leaders in the Christian world.

According to church historian Eusebius, the slave Onesimus on whose behalf the apostle Paul wrote a letter to his master Philemon, became the *episkopos* of the Ephesian church. That word is often translated 'bishop,' but to Christians of the first couple of centuries the term meant something different — an *episkopos* was literally an overseer. That Christian leader was responsible not only for spiritual direction, but also economic and manufacturing expertise. In secular life an *episkopos* was often the slave who was the overseer of the economic well-being of his master's holdings. This would have been a natural fit for Onesimus.

Paul avoided the opportunity of claiming a superior status for himself, not even when it would have kept him out of prison or saved him from a beating. It wasn't until there was a riot in Jerusalem that lead the tribune to decide that Paul should be flayed alive with a lashing from a whip whose thongs were wrapped around metal and stone that Paul said those three magic words, "Civis Romanum sum." I am a Roman citizen! (See Acts 22:25) His default setting was to say with regard to his many accomplishments that he considered everything else dung "in order that I may gain Christ " (Philippians 38).What does this mean to us? What does this mean to receive others like that child, and in doing so treat them like Jesus?

One former slave, who became a leader of a late first-century church and who wrote a massive book, "The Shepherd of Hermas," that was so popular it almost made the cut for the New Testament, said about those who are pure in heart:

> *They are veritable infants, whose hearts do not invent evil, who hardly know what corruption is and who have remained childlike forever. People such as these, therefore, undoubtedly dwell in the kingdom of God, because they in no way defile God's commandments, but have continued in innocence all the days of their lives in the same state of mind ("The Shepherd of Hermas" 3-9-39).*

What was Jesus telling us? First of all, leadership is servanthood. Whoever would be the greatest should be the greatest servant, and the servant of all, those who are poor as well as those who are rich, the humble as well as the haughty, the introvert as well as the extrovert, those who are hard to serve as well as those to whom it is easy to reach out.

It also means standing up for those who have no one to stand up for them. In today's world many of us romanticize childhood as a happy, unsullied time, and perhaps it is for our children. As the church we should be happy to make children feel welcome, instead of simply scolding them and forcing to "behave," which usually means being silent and unmoving.

But let us not forget that children are still the most vulnerable members of our society. Children are exploited economically, forced to work as slaves in factories and fields. Children are physically abused, often with no consequences to their abusers since they have no voice. Children are the victims of sexual abuse and are kidnapped into sex slavery. We should make the protection of children a great priority for the church and for us individually.

It's too easy to, like the disciples, ignore the cross and argue about who's the greatest. Christians jockey for positions of power within the church instead of cheerfully outdoing each other in service to each other and the world.

Just as Jesus was teaching his disciples about his death and resurrection, so he was teaching us about what his death and resurrection means — that if we wish to welcome Christ in our lives, we ought to be ready to welcome the least in the world's eyes into the kingdom of God. We must wash each other's feet. We must reach out to the least of these.

Amen.

For Us Or Against Us?

There's a scrap of papyrus (a form of paper made from reeds that grew in the Nile) that has survived the centuries until it was found in the Egyptian desert over a century ago. Although there are gaps in the piece, enough has survived to make it clear what it is.

It's a list of Olympic champions.

The Greek Olympic games were held every four years for a thousand years. The list includes champions for all the events including the 200 yard dash which was the oldest event in the games. This list included champions for boxing, wrestling, a no-holds-barred event called the Pankraton, chariot races, the long jump, the discus, the javelin, and the Pentathlon. Some names appear more than once, champions who reigned over decades. Some appear once.

Each victor received plenty of prizes: land, slaves, gold, and in some cases a lifetime pension from the city from which he hailed. They also received a victor's crown and lasting glory. Poets wrote poems in their honor. Artists and sculptors immortalized their accomplishments.

There's only one thing missing on this piece of papyrus — there are no awards for second or third place. There's no honorable mention. You are either the champion, or you're nothing.

To the ancient Greeks athletic competitions had one winner. Everyone else was a loser. But in our day we honor more than just the first place finisher. We also admire those who try, who compete, who push themselves farther than they thought they could go.

The Christian rewards are for everyone. There's a bumper sticker that reads: "Second Place is First Loser." That is not the Christian attitude. — not 2,000 years ago — not now.

The apostle Paul referred to that victor's crown handed out in the Olympics when he talked about having fought the good fight, ran the good race, and added: "From now on there is reserved for me the crown of righteousness, which the Lord, the righteous judge, will give me on that day, and not only to me but also to all who have longed for his appearing (Philippians 4:8)." That sounds like a lot of winners. And when John the Revelator looks into the heavens from the prison island of Patmos he saw "… a great multitude that no one could count, from every nation, from all tribes and peoples and languages, standing before the throne and before the Lamb, robed in white, with palm branches in their hands (Revelation 7:9)." Oddly enough, sometimes the faithful in both the Old Testament and the New Testament don't share this attitude.

In Numbers 11:26-29, Moses gathered seventy elders around the tabernacle and the Lord's Spirit filled the elders with a spirit of prophecy. There were two men who remained behind, Eldad and Medad, who were also filled with the Spirit and who also displayed the spirit of prophecy. A young man who witnessed this ran to where Moses stood and told him all about it, and Joshua, normally a level headed person, said, "My lord Moses, stop them (Numbers 11:28)!" And Moses responded: "Are you jealous for my sake? Would that all the Lord's people were prophets, and that the LORD would put his Spirit on them (Numbers 11:29)! "

John, who was one of the three apostles that was with Jesus when he was transfigured, (and perhaps he thought he was special because he'd been up on the mountaintop) reported, like Joshua: "Teacher, we saw someone casting out demons in your name, and we tried to stop him, because he was not following us (John 9:38)." Jesus, like Moses, was not interested in stopping those outside his inner circle from doing great works. "Do not stop him; for no one who does a deed of power in my name will be able soon afterward to speak evil of me. Whoever is not against us is for us (Mark 9:39-40)." It is important to know that this passage follows a larger discussion about which disciple is the greatest (9:33-37). Jesus said that, "Whoever wants to be first must be last of all and servant of all (Mark 9:35)." He then took up a child in his arms. Children were not valued as they are today – they gained value as they grew able to work. Children did not have first access to resources. But Jesus took this marginalized member of society and said, "Whoever welcomes one such child in my name welcomes me, and whoever welcomes me welcomes not me but the one who sent me (9:37)."

Having described a situation in which servanthood and acceptance of the marginalized are the true hallmarks of a disciple, can there be any wonder that in the context of this story Jesus would expect his disciples to abandon jealousy and rivalry for inclusion and acceptance?

When the disciples told Jesus they had stopped an outsider from healing others in the name of Jesus, Jesus responded, "Whoever is not against us is for us. For truly I tell you, whoever gives you a cup of water to drink because you bear the name of Christ will by no means lose the reward (9:40-41)."

A cup of cold water in the name of Jesus? It sounds a lot like Matthew 25, where Jesus at the last judgment told those who fed, clothed, visited or gave a drink to the least of these did it for Jesus.

Now oddly enough, in that same gospel of Matthew, Jesus said just the opposite of what he said here. In Matthew's gospel he was reported to have said that whoever is not for us is against us.

But the situation was totally different. Jesus had been challenged in several successive stories by religious authorities who accused him and his followers of acting against the faith, and they finally went so far as to claim that the work of Jesus was demonic.

Matthew described a situation where the criticism of Jesus had gone beyond the pale to the point where he was literally demonized. (This describes the situation we often encounter in modern political and religious debate, where opponents are not debated but demonized also.)

In this context Jesus said, "Whoever is not with me is against me, and whoever does not gather with me scatters. Therefore I tell you, people will be forgiven for every sin and blasphemy, but blasphemy against the Spirit will not be forgiven (Matthew 12:30-31)."

Context is key. Jesus probably said both things. That's how wisdom sayings work — they have to be understood in the context in which they are spoken, and they are not one size fits all. What is wisdom in one circumstance is folly in another.

On the one hand as Christians it is important that we accept others who are doing the work of Jesus, and be prepared to accept a cup of cold water from them rather than rejecting them for not measuring up to our standards, especially when they threaten our own imagined place in the gospel kingdom.

On the other hand Matthew's version warns us those who demonize their opponents, who demean and dismiss others, are in danger of blaspheming against that Spirit that is present in all of us.

The Bible, after all, is not a convenient tool to back up our own already established notions. It is the living word of God.

There was a time when everyone assumed their own denomination was the one true church and everyone else in every Christian denomination was going to hell. We're not even talking, as Jesus suggested, about people who are not his followers. He had no other followers at that point.

Now during that same period a whole generation was inspired to take the gospel throughout the world. Young people became missionaries and preached about Jesus in different countries, far from home, far from the comforts of those homes, far from family and friends.

For the most part, the missionaries didn't take their denominational bickering to the front lines of evangelism. They worked together because they recognized far from home that the things that separated them were not as important as they were led to believe! They realized they were one in Christ.

It's the same when we're engaged in ecumenical ministries like soup kitchens, domestic violence shelters, community programs for children, and the like. At a time like that, we have to say, as Jesus did, that whoever is not against us is for us. We don't ask for a litmus test, and thank heavens, the needs are so great that no one asks us if we measure up either. We're simply broken people helping other broken people, sharing a cup of cold water in the name of Jesus.

Pay attention. People outside our church, even outside our faith, may be doing God's work, and we should not stop it. The front lines of ministry are no place for protecting what we imagine is our territory. We'll leave it for God to decide who's saved. After all, the harvest is plentiful but the workers are few.

But Jesus has more to say in this passage and it is stark.

"If any of you put a stumbling block before one of these little ones who believe in me, it would be better for you if a great millstone were hung around your neck and you were thrown into the sea. If your hand causes you to stumble, cut it off; it is better for you to enter life maimed than to have two hands and to

go to hell, to the unquenchable fire. And if your foot causes you to stumble, cut it off; it is better for you to enter life lame than to have two feet and to be thrown into hell. And if your eye causes you to stumble, tear it out; it is better for you to enter the kingdom of God with one eye than to have two eyes and to be thrown into hell, where their worm never dies, and the fire is never quenched (9:42-48)."

Part of the Jewish story-telling technique is hyperbole, or exaggeration. It would be a mistake to cut off a hand, a foot, or an eye without talking to your pastor first and consider the possibility of seeking forgiveness. Those who easily despair probably don't need to hear these verses.

Nor is Jesus exactly talking about hell. He talks about Gehenna, a trash heap outside the city that is constantly smoldering. Gehenna was south of Jerusalem, a city dump, garbage was burned, maggots ate animal entrails, flames always smoldered (see Isaiah 66:24) not eternal damnation but utter annihilation. This is about obliteration — obliteration if one harms a "little one."

Jesus is using this term not only for children, the most vulnerable members of society, but also the most vulnerable in our midst. That includes people with post-traumatic stress disorder, degenerative diseases, emotional handicaps, senior citizens, those unable to make reasoned choices, leaving them vulnerable to those who want to take advantage of them — you make your own list. People who prey upon others must heed that warning about a giant millstone. These are the people who need to hear that whoever is not for Jesus is against him, so they know when they harm the vulnerable, they show they are against Jesus.

These verses are not for those who are suffering, who can't make sense of their lives, who need to know that despite their confusion, if they are not against Jesus, Jesus already takes their side.

Finally, Jesus talks about salt — salt is both a seasoning and a preservative. It was connected with rites of purification and ritual offerings in Leviticus. We are salted by the obstacles we have encountered and sometimes overcome. We are salted by our service in the name of Christ, and in our offerings.

"Have salt in yourselves, and be at peace with one another (Mark 9:50)." Jesus tells us. Know that we are all salted, all broken in different ways, and yet in our suffering and struggles we are on the side of Jesus, and we are fit for service in his name.

Don't sweat the small stuff that separates us as believers from one another. We are on a great team! We are part of the Lord's people. We are one in Christ.

Amen.

For Men Only?

In the year 311 BC a marriage contract in Egypt was drawn up for Heraclides and Demetria, both from the town of Koan.

The contract specified that the bride was bringing into the marriage clothing and bling worth a thousand drachmas. Heraclides, meanwhile, agreed to support Demetria according to what was fitting for a freeborn woman. As to where the two of them would live, that would be whatever they both agreed to after consulting with each other.

This marriage, like some that we read about, also had prenuptial conditions, as far as divorce was concerned. If Demetria did not act in an appropriate manner, Heraclides could send her away without any of the wealth she'd brought into the marriage but only — and this was key, if three men agreed he was right, and both husband and wife had to agree on this three person panel!

Conversely, if Heraclides brought in other women to live in the house to shame Demetria, or had children by other women, or if he wronged Demetria in any way whatsoever she would not only keep the wealth she brought into the relationship but he would have to give her an extra thousand drachmas. Once again, a three person panel was involved, and both sides had to approve the arbitrators.

Unlike many marriage customs around the world, not only in the ancient past but in the present, that give all the power to men and none to women, these two Egyptian free-born people seem to have entered into an agreement where there were safeguards to protect both of them.

Certainly it doesn't sound as if women had any degree of mutual protection in biblical times, judging from the way the Pharisees describe the law of Moses.

Or did they?

This present scripture has been used in the past to guarantee almost a master/slave relationship between husbands and wives. It has been used to force women to stay in abusive relationships. It has meant, in practical terms, that in some churches those who are divorced against their own wish find they cannot be a part of the life of the church they grew up in. They become pariahs, and in the end are driven away from the church.

What did Jesus mean by these words? What do these words really mean?

Perhaps a clue is to be found in the second part of today's gospel passage where the subject shifts from the rights of wives, or the lack of them, to the place of children in the kingdom of God. Because, as we will see, Jesus is speaking about two very vulnerable groups, who at that time, and in most times, had very few legal protections.

Let's look at the first part first. The passage as we have it seems simple enough. Jesus is busy teaching the people when some Pharisees came to ask him a question with the specific intention of testing him and trapping him. To a certain extent they did not really care about the answer. They simply hoped that whatever Jesus said, aye or nay, would give them sufficient grounds for condemning Jesus on the charge that he did not follow the law of Moses.

Note that the incident begins with the phrase "*Some* Pharisees...". Some Christians seem to think that *all* Pharisees were villains, evil Bible misinterpreters who tried to hold people in the chains of legalistic interpretations of scripture.

This is simply untrue. We're only talking about the stinkers here. If we lived in first century Judea, we would have attended a synagogue which was administered by a leader who was a Pharisee. Our pastor would probably have been a Pharisee. He would have been the person who stood up for us, preached on the scriptures for us, and looked after our spiritual needs. Unlike Sadducees who had little interest in common people, or the communal societies like the Essenes which raised the bar very high when it came to standards of behavior, we would have found the Pharisees to be our kind of people.

These particular Pharisees, at any rate, seemed to be recognizing Jesus had authority when it came to interpreting scripture, for they asked him a question about the law of Moses — "Is it lawful for a man to divorce his wife?"

Though it seems like a compliment, they were of course trying to trap him. And Jesus, as he did on more than one occasion, answered a question with a question. "What did Moses command you?" By Moses, Jesus is referring to the Torah, the first five books of our Bible. These ancient books told the history of the people and gave case law. To Jesus' question these Pharisees gave a simple reply: "Moses allowed a man to write a certificate of dismissal and to divorce her."

They were referring to Deuteronomy 24:1-5. I'm going to read you the first two verses of this passage. I'll read the other three verses in a few minutes, for reasons you'll understand a little later.

Suppose a man enters into marriage with a woman, but she does not please him because he finds something objectionable about her, and so he writes her a certificate of divorce, puts it in her hand, and sends her out of his house; she then leaves his house and goes off to become another man's wife.

The law seems to be very clear — if the man decides for whatever reason he wants a divorce, he gets a divorce. It is cut and dried. What's to argue about?

But if you read the law of Moses from beginning to end you'll begin to notice something odd — there's no wedding service in the Bible. Weddings took place, and were probably performed according to custom, but most of the words that may have been spoken at your own wedding, or a wedding you attended have come from human custom and practice.

The same is true when it comes to divorce. Divorce took place among God's people, again according to the customs that had developed among them, but the references to divorce in the law and the prophets only indirectly referred to these practices. This particular scripture speaks to only a few specific incidents.

These Pharisees were literally taking what was meant to be case law for a specific instance and applying it literally and universally.

Poet and scholar Robert Alter, in his translation of the Torah, rendered the phrase "something objectionable" as "he finds in her some shamefully exposed thing.." The Jewish Publication Society's translation said "he finds something obnoxious" about her. Duane L. Christensen's translation for the Word Biblical Commentary is very literal: "...because he finds in her 'a naked thing...'" The implication is that she is engaged in public lewd and sexual misbehavior. It has nothing to do with whether she has failed to please her husband in the ordinary course of events.

So there's more than meets the eye in this passage. Deuteronomy goes on to say:

> *Then suppose the second man dislikes her, writes*
> *her a bill of divorce, puts it in her hand, and sends*
> *her out of his house (or the second man who married*
> *her dies); her first husband, who sent her away, is not*

permitted to take her again to be his wife after she has been defiled; for that would be abhorrent to the Lord, and you shall not bring guilt on the land that the Lord your God is giving you as a possession.

Some commentators suggest that this passage in its entirety is stating that men could not divorce their wives, marry another, then divorce that wife and remarry the first wife as a way of swapping wives and still staying within custom and law. This piece of case law goes even further. Deuteronomy 24:5 says, *"When a man is newly married, he shall not go out with the army or be charged with any related duty. He shall be free at home one year, to be happy with the wife whom he has married."*

This addition to the law about divorce is designed to stop people from divorcing their current wife, then temporarily marrying another woman, in order to avoid military service, and then remarrying their first wife. So far from giving men *carte blanche* to divorce wives casually, this law prevented them from divorcing to swap wives or dodge the draft.

Jesus knew this. Jesus knew scripture. He ought to. Jesus also knew that the Hebrew words were referring to extraordinarily lewd public behavior, so he replied, scornfully one imagines, that this law had more to do with their hardness of heart — something we associate with the tyranny of a Pharaoh, than permission to divorce as one pleased.

Jesus, as elsewhere, pushed the law to its limit for these individuals, and in doing so fulfilled the law, as he put it elsewhere. Remember the Sermon on the Mount? Jesus said "You have heard it said..." and told those listening that while the law forbade murder, those who insulted their brothers and sisters were murdering the self-esteem and integrity of another human being, through their verbal abuse. He said that the law forbade adultery, but those who lusted in their heart were committing adultery as well. He said that the law told us to love our neighbors, and that even our enemies were our neighbors, and we were to love them too.

Jesus goes back further than Deuteronomy, all the way to the deeps of time and creation. Genesis goes back farther than Moses. Jesus showed that marriage is hallowed by God at the beginning of time, and therefore those who interpret this law from Deuteronomy as something that allowed them to divorce a spouse for the slightest reason were opening themselves up to the charge of adultery. He therefore created a whole new case law for those who thought they could dispose of women on a whim. They couldn't.

Later, when his disciples in private seemed to worriedly ask about this, Jesus repeated what he had said. Whoever divorced their spouse and remarried is an adulterer.

More insight can be gained by looking at the next four verses of today's passage. People brought little children to Jesus, hoping for even a touch from the master's hand, and the disciples, like many church busybodies, did their best to keep the children at bay, but Jesus, when he saw this, responded indignantly, "Let the little children come to me; do not stop them; for it is to such as these that the kingdom of God belongs."

At the time of Jesus, children represented one of the most vulnerable populations. They had no rights, and relatively little value, until they were able to share in the family's craft or agriculture. They were expected to work, and until they worked, they were a waste of time for someone like Jesus, at least in the eyes of the apostles. But Jesus told us that those on the margins of society — little children, women, women who have been divorced — are ones God favors. God's law protects them. God's people ought to encourage them.

When Jesus said "Truly I tell you, whoever does not receive the kingdom of God as a little child will never enter it," he may not have been saying what we usually think he was saying — that there is something pure and innocent about childhood and we need to bring that to the table. No, Jesus was saying that in order to be part of God's people we can't act like God owes us anything, as if we were workers paid by the hour or by the job.

Jesus was suggesting that despite our high opinion of ourselves we have no apparent monetary value, much like children before they're able to help with the family business. Therefore we all, whether we have a high opinion of ourselves or not, depend on God's grace. All of us are in that position of being given the priceless gift as a child — our value comes from God's estimation, and not the work we do.

That is what that whole grace thing is about.

If you want a good example of what Jesus thinks about the divorced — see the story about the woman at the well, in the gospel of John. This woman had been married five times, and she wasn't legally married to her current beaux. Yet Jesus asked her for a drink of water, demonstrating that whatever barriers his society put up against the two of them conversing he was willing to ignore. Jesus offered her the living water, which would sustain her spiritually. And this woman became the evangelist that brought her whole village into the fold.

The truth is, just like that marriage contract I referred to at the beginning of this message, God's people had worked out over the centuries equitable ways to protect people in marriage, and to protect them in divorce as well.

Divorce is never a great outcome. No one goes into a wedding thinking, "If this doesn't work out I'll just bail on the whole marriage thing." But there are abusers and there are abused people, and no one has the right to tyrannize another human being. In our own time we are recognizing that those who are terrorized, abused, and misused, male or female, have a right to begin anew.

Rather than being hard-hearted, at least until we ourselves are forced to throw ourselves before the throne of mercy for much-needed grace, let us offer each other kindness and understanding. Let us dedicate ourselves to protecting the most vulnerable in our society This is how it was in the beginning, is now, and ever shall be, in the kingdom of grace and good news.

Amen.

Pulling Our Punches

Nobel Prize Laureate for Literature Robert Allan Zimmerman — more popularly known as Bob Dylan — has written many memorable lyrics. He has a good ear for the rhythms of speech, poetry, and the Bible. In his song "The Times They Are A-Changin'" Dylan listed a number of factors that should prove to those who stand in the way of truth that "*Your order is rapidly fadin'.*" He concluded with words that echo Jesus —

"For the first one now will later be last, for the times, they are a-changin'."

In the gospels it is clear that Jesus was turning the world upside down, and those who are the least, the lost, and the last will be first in the kingdom of God. In the gospels of Matthew and Luke this becomes clear in the Beatitudes: the meek will inherit the earth. The poor, and the poor in spirit, are the most blessed.

Mark's is the shortest of the four gospels. This is the longest of the discourses in the shortest gospel and it is on economics and material possessions. It couldn't be clearer than it is expressed here, that money can greatly hinder us when we seek to follow Jesus. Although, as we shall see, over the centuries many well-intentioned preachers and teachers have tried to water this down.

Maybe the world has a better handle on this than many Christians. Commercials tell us we need more, more, more.

Music videos feature artists whose fingers are covered with golden rings. Sober-faced financial advisers assure us that with proper management we can ensure that there will be more — more money for our retirement, and for our children and grandchildren.

There's nothing necessarily evil about any of this. All of us worry about our economic futures.

But Jesus is calling us to look at the world, and economics, in an upside down way. No doubt, money when it is not idolized is very important. Our eternal destiny is even more so.

Some people would rather separate economics and worship into two different categories, two kingdoms. But if you read through the entire Bible you can't help but notice how sacrifice was central to worship in the temple, and how the prophets railed against the rich and powerful preying upon the poor and weak..

This passage begins with Jesus setting out on a journey — the first steps it seems on the path to Jerusalem, where Jesus will give all to save all. But in the gospel of Mark it seems like every time Jesus sets out to go somewhere there someone is in need — the leader of a synagogue whose daughter is ill, a woman who has spent all her money seeking for a cure and who has no one left to turn to but Jesus, a centurion with a sick servant — and as we shall see here, a rich young man who's on the right track already.

Mark told us: "…a man ran up and knelt before him…". A man with the wealth this individual has can usually employ someone to do the running for him, but we have to be impressed that he takes off with speed to catch up with Jesus and stop him. It's admirable that he doesn't worry about how this would look. And at the end of his run, perhaps breathless, he knelt before Jesus, showing him more honor than most in positions of authority showed to him.

"Good Teacher, what must I do to inherit eternal life?" Addressing Jesus as teacher shows extraordinary respect. As for calling him "Good Teacher," there is no example before the first century AD of anyone using such an address.

Give the rich young man credit. His question is a legitimate one, on human terms. It was not asked to trap Jesus, but assumed Jesus knew the answer. It was the question a disciple would ask of a teacher.

Which makes the answer of our Lord a little odd, at first. "Why do you call me good? No one is good but God alone."

Ahhh...

Jesus *is* the Son of God, and we'd think he shared in God's goodness, but the young man had asked a human-oriented question, and it demanded an answer from a human point of view. It is a human question, but as we shall see, there is no human answer.

The divine point of view is implicit in the way Jesus answered the question: which commandment is the greatest? You will remember that Jesus famously replied with two commandments, one from Deuteronomy 6:5 and one from Leviticus 19:18 — *You shall love the Lord your God with all your heart,* soul, *strength, and mind, and you shall love your neighbor as yourself.* The commandment from Deuteronomy begins with the call to worship known as the Shema, from the commanding word for Hear! or Listen! *Hear, O Israel, the Lord your God, the Lord is one!*

When the young man addressed the divine teacher in a human fashion he may have been forgetting the opening commandments Moses brought down from Mount Sinai, about there being only one God, and how it is required we have no graven images or no God before our God.

This helps explain the response of Jesus:

> *You know the commandments: 'You shall not murder; You shall not commit adultery; You shall not steal; You shall not bear false witness; You shall not defraud; Honor your father and mother.'"*

The commandments he mentioned were the "horizontal" commandments. The "vertical" commandments concern the relationship between God above and we humans below. The "horizontal" commandments concern the relationships we have with the people all around us. These are the ones implicit in the Second Command Jesus called the greatest — *you shall love your neighbor as yourself.*

This is how we are to treat humans. This is the human answer. The human answer is correct.

It is to his credit that the rich young man could answer: "Teacher, I have kept all these since my youth."

And this is where the rich young man fell short.

This was all well and good, but it was centered in the young man's desire to "do." What must I "do" the young man asked. This is a pretty good start, but in a real sense we can't *do* enough. The love of God is ours, and the love of God is unearned.

Mark told us that Jesus loved him. One translation reads "Jesus loved him at first sight…" and that deep and abiding love, the kind of love that Jesus seems to have for all of us, lead him to challenge this person to go even farther.

So he said: "You lack one thing; go, sell what you own, and give the money to the poor, and you will have treasure in heaven; then come, follow me."

Go. Sell. Give. Come. Follow. Five commands in the imperative. Liquidate your assets. Evidently Jesus knew something about him he did not know himself — his wealth. Once again Jesus, the Lord of life, did not respond with pieties — he asked for everything. Jesus wants all of us.

I don't know about you, but this is where I start squirming. This is where I look for a way out. Jesus was speaking to the rich young man. *He* needed to go, sell, give, come, and follow. In the ancient world the enormous gap between the rich and poor meant that *he* needed to go this extra step. *I* don't need to.

Jesus, isn't it time for us to start speaking about prayer and meekness and stuff like that? Can't we just back off the economics a little bit?

Hold on to that bar in front of you because this roller coaster is about to get worse.

It says, "When he heard this, he was shocked and went away grieving, for he had many possessions."

The word translated as "shocked" is a rare one, *stuynazo*. It can be translated as angry, in the sense of weather. In Matthew 16:3 it is used to mean "an angry sky." We might say, "His face clouded up." The rich young man's physical appearance betrayed an emotion that made it clear that Jesus had asked him to do the one thing he could not do.

This young man, who *ran* to catch up to Jesus, *walked* away dejected, knowing he could not possibly do this. In a way, isn't this impossible? Think if this was preached in every congregation in every church in this country — and everyone did it. First of all, all the folks on the finance committee would have to wonder how we were going to pay for air conditioning, heating, lighting, or much less things like our missions programs.

And second, someone has to grow crops, manufacture goods, and keep the world running on an even keel.

And yet, and yet —

Augustine looked at this passage as one that was really doable! He wrote:

I who write this have greatly loved the total devotion of which the Lord spoke when he once said to the rich young man: "Go, sell what you have and give to the poor, and come, follow me" I have so loved it that I have indeed acted upon it myself, not by my own strength but by his assisting grace. The apostles were the first to follow in the practice of this complete self-giving. One who gives up both what one owns and what one desires to own, gives up the whole world. (Letters, 157, To Hilarius.)

You'd think Jesus would turn to his disciples and give them some reassurance, but what followed was this:

> *Then Jesus looked around and said to his disciples, "How hard it will be for those who have wealth to enter the kingdom of God!" And the disciples were perplexed at these words. But Jesus said to them again, "Children, how hard it is to enter the kingdom of God! It is easier for a camel to go through the eye of a needle than for someone who is rich to enter the kingdom of God."*

Okay, the difficult has just become impossible. Oh, over the centuries preachers in the pulpit have tried to help Jesus pull his punches. They'd tell that there is a gate going into Jerusalem called "the eye of the needle," because it was so narrow, and before a camel could be walked through that entrance merchants would have to remove *some* of its cargo. Not all, just some. And, of course, this meant that all of us must divest ourselves of *some* of our goods, not all. Whew! What a relief.

Well, that story is only as old as the Middle Ages. It's told today by tour guides to gullible tourists, perhaps hoping for his listeners to remove some of their camel's cargo and give them a nice tip. But there was no gate known as the eye of the needle in ancient times. It's just a sneaky way of making the impossible possible.

I must add that one of the story telling techniques of Jesus was exaggeration, or hyperbole. This is a funny comeback. The image of a camel trying to get through the eye of a needle probably made the first listeners to this little one-line parable laugh, especially because it made the rich uncomfortable.

The disciples got it — if this was true, who could be saved?

And we already know the answer — on the basis of what we do — no one. *No one* — not without God's love. Not without God's grace.

Not without the cross.

This is hard for us to hear, because we expect to be able to do everything by ourselves, without help from anybody. We make independence and self-reliance a modern idol which is every bit a false god as the golden calf made by God's people while Moses was up on the mountain.

This is hard for us to hear, because none of us measures up. Every one of us is holding on to something we don't want to give up. We don't intend to give up.

We have to ask — was Jesus even able to do this? Although he complained that birds had nests and foxes had dens, but the Son of Man had no place to lay his head, we know from Luke 8:1-3 that Mary Magdalene, Salome, Joanna, and other women supported his ministry financially, out of the money they controlled. We know that Paul might have complained about his sufferings in all his travels, but in places like Corinth he set up shop with his friends Priscilla and Aquila and showed his economic good sense by using the tools of his trade to make tents and support his own ministry financially.

Don't we need to practice some measure of financial smarts in order to have money to contribute to the needs of the poor, the suffering, the refugees, and the lost?

Don't denominational staffs go out of their way to encourage people to plan for the future so they can donate large sums at the end of their lives to the support of a beloved church?

This is where salvation by grace comes into play. "Jesus looked at them and said, "For mortals it is impossible, but not for God; for God all things are possible."

That's the place to where we need to come. If we rely on human righteousness alone we are stuck. But we need not do so. We are saved by grace.

That grace assures us that we have a heavenly reward. When Peter told Jesus that they had left everything to follow him, Jesus responded that those who have given up everything will get everything, and, as he concluded "...and in the age to come eternal life."

In other words, our stuff isn't really our stuff. If we truly follow Jesus, in a sense we've already left it behind. We are only stewards of the world's wealth. We can enjoy it — but we own things, they don't own us.

That might have been the rich young man's mistake. He thought eternal life could be earned — but it is freely given by the Savior of the world.

Even so, that doesn't get us off the hook. It is prudent to save money for our future, and for the futures of our children and grandchildren. It is prudent to build homes and accumulate wealth, and like Joseph advised Pharaoh, take advantage of good years to prepare for lean years.

Still, as one of the ancient fathers of the church, Salvian the Presbyter, wrote, "There is no compelling necessity for you to store up large earthly treasures for your children. You would do better to make your offspring treasures of God than make them richer in worldly goods."

You can't separate Christianity and economics. These are not separate categories. So let us ask ourselves right now: What is the one thing you need to do? What is holding you back. Is it small? Is it large?

So we come full circle, recognizing that the times, they are a-changing! Jesus, at the end of this passage, assured his disciples, "But many who are first will be last, and the last will be first." There is a changing of the order. We who live in this country are wealthy beyond the dreams of most people in the world. If we put our heart and soul into what we own instead of what we believe, we who live in the First world may find ourselves last while those from the poorer nations, or the poor who dwell in our midst will find themselves first.

Take heart. With God all things are possible.

Take seriously the command to go, sell, give, come, and follow!

Amen.

(The quotations from Augustine and Salvian comes from *Ancient Christian Commentary on Scripture, New Testament II Mark*, p 145.)

Are Ye Able?

Although Christianity was an illegal religion during much of the first three centuries of the faith, there were both times when authorities turned a blind eye to their existence, and other times when persecution was intensified.

During the reign of the Emperor Trajan (98-117AD) persecution intensified. In 108 AD, one of those arrested and condemned to be thrown to the wild beasts for the entertainment of the cheering crowds was Ignatius, the overseer of the church at Antioch.

Antioch had been a center of the Christian faith from the early days of the apostles. It was at Antioch that the term 'Christian' was first used. But though Ignatius was arrested, tried, and sentenced in Antioch, he was sent by ship to Rome to meet his fate.

As was the custom, the ship that transported him in the Mediterranean Sea probably hugged the coast and docked every night for safety's sake. All along the way he seemed to have received delegations of Christians dockside. We know this because he was allowed to write letters that he used to encourage the church folks he met on his journey.

In his letter to the Romans, written to the church at his ultimate destination, he encouraged them to pray for him so he could prove he was able to meet his appointment with the wild beasts.

He asked them "This one thing — pray for me to be strong inwardly and outwardly, in order that I not only speak, but have the will, so that I will not only be called a Christian, but be found one" (Romans 3.2). Complaining of his treatment by the ten fierce guards who kept watch over him, he said he longed for the wild beasts to tear him apart so that he could attain Jesus Christ. Seeming to echo the prison letters of Paul, he wrote at one point: "I will profit nothing from the world, nor the kingdoms of this world. It is better to die in Christ Jesus compared to being king over the ends of the earth. I am zealous for him who died for us. I long for he who rose for us. Birth pangs are upon me."

Ignatius took seriously the words of Jesus to his apostles that they would share his suffering. Ignatius was willing to die for Christ. Like the hymn written by C. Michael Hawn nearly a century ago asks and answers:

> *"Are ye able?" said the Master to be crucified with me?*
> *"Yes," the sturdy dreamers answered, to the death we follow thee."*
> *Lord, we are able. Our spirits are thine. Remold them, make us, like thee, divine.*
> *Thy guiding radiance above us shall be a beacon to God, to love, and loyalty.*
> *(in the public domain)*

Ignatius spoke about earnestly desiring to share in the way of Jesus. In today's Bible passage the disciples want a spot next to Jesus. They just don't quite yet understand exactly what that meant.

Mark wrote that James and John, the sons of Zebedee, came to Jesus with a request — that he grant them whatever they asked of him.

That kind of request probably got alarm bells ringing and red flags waving. Parents know that when a kid requests that, they are probably going to be asked to do something they'd never do otherwise!

Jesus patiently asked them what that might be, and the two replied, "Grant us to sit, one at your right hand and one at your left, in your glory (Mark 10:37).

Now these two have been with Peter and Jesus on some special occasions — they were there at the Mount of Transfiguration, and they were also together for the raising of Jairus' daughter. They would also be together to ask Jesus for information about the coming tribulation and end of the world.

The two of them, known by the nickname the *Sons of Thunder*, may have been loud and boisterous, so it's no surprise that the other ten apostles heard what they said about having places of honor when Jesus comes into his glory. Jesus squelched their jealousy.

> *But Jesus said to them, "You do not know what you are asking. Are you able to drink the cup that I drink, or be baptized with the baptism that I am baptized with (10:38)?*

Jesus had been speaking very openly about his coming arrest and death at the hands of the authorities, but the two did not seem to have understood what Jesus was talking about. Neither had the others.

Give James and John credit. Whether they understood fully or not, they said that they were able to drink this cup, to which Jesus assured them, "The cup that I drink you will drink; and with the baptism with which I am baptized, you will be baptized..." (10:39). Jesus went on to say that those spots were not for him to pass out, but the one who sent him. Still, the apostles were going to learn firsthand that the road to glory is filled with suffering and triumph. You can't bypass the suffering.

James would be martyred in the early 40's, beheaded by Herod Antipas (see Acts 12:2). We don't know if John the apostle was martyred, but it seems likely from the tone used in the gospel of Mark that the prophecy came true.

Actually, if you think about it, the first two given places at his right hand and left hand at his moment of glory were the two rebels crucified with Jesus.

This led Jesus to share a crucial point in his lesson. After the other ten reacted angrily at the request by John and James:

> *Jesus called them and said to them, "You know that among the Gentiles those whom they recognize as their rulers lord it over them, and their great ones are tyrants over them. But it is not so among you; but whoever wishes to become great among you must be your servant, and whoever wishes to be first among you must be slave of all. For the Son of Man came not to be served but to serve, and to give his life a ransom for many (Mark 10: 42-45)."*

In the Roman world the great ones so-called not only lorded it over others, but lesser people went out of their way to flatter them to a sickening degree. To be willing to serve, and be slave to all, after the manner of Jesus, was the path chosen by many of the martyrs. Augustine, the fourth-century African theologian told the Christians under his care, many of whom would be martyred in their time:

> *Ponder how profound this is. They were conferring with him about glory. He intended to precede loftiness with humility and, only through humility to ready the way for loftiness itself. For, of course, even those disciples who wanted to sit, the one on his right, the other on his left, were looking to glory. They were on the lookout, but did not see by what way. In order that they might come to their homeland*

in due order, the Lord called them back to the Narrow
way. For the homeland is on high and the way to it is
lowly. The homeland is life in Christ; the way is dy-
ing with Christ. The way is suffering with Christ; the
goal is abiding with him eternally. Why do you seek
the homeland if you are not seeking the way to it?
(Augustine, Sermons on the Gospel of John 28.5.2)

There's a book of over 1,100 pages found in nearly every Amish home — it's full title is "The Bloody Theater or The Martyrs Mirror of the Defenseless Christians Who Baptized Only Upon Confession of Faith, and Who Suffered and Died for the Testimony of Jesus, Their Savior, From the Time of Christ to the Year A.D. 1600." Known more simply as the Martyr's Mirror, this book recounts the martyrs of Christianity's early centuries, as well as the thousands who were martyred by so-called fellow Christians because they refused to attend the official state churches, but met to worship in their homes, and were baptized as adults rather than infants.

Just as most of those murdered by Islamic terrorists are their fellow Muslims, in the same way so many Christians have been martyred by fellow Christians.

One of the stories from the book concerns Jan Portier of Flanders. It describes the brutal tortures used upon him, and tells how he and others were sentenced in 1568 to be strangled and their bodies burnt. However there were companies of Spanish soldiers stationed in the city, and the commander-in-chief commanded that they be burned alive.

When the brethren heard that they were to be
burnt alive, they raised their voices and sang: "I call
upon thee, O heavenly Father." Then the Spaniards
beat them so dreadfully with sticks that the eye of
one fell out on his cheek. And thus they were burnt
alive, the Spaniards loudly vociferating, and throw-

*ing sticks in the fire at a rapid rate, as desiring to
have part in this madness, as though they thought to
do God service thereby.*

In the book *Amish Grace,* which concerns the criminal
assault on the West Nickel Mines Amish School, resulting in
the shooting of eight children, and the death of five of them,
along with the suicide of the shooter, the authors talk about
the effect stories from the *Martyr's Mirror* had on the way
the children tried to save others, and how the Amish community was determined to forgive the murderer, after the manner of Jesus. Amish are often harassed and reviled by some
of their neighbors for living a different lifestyle. They are
sometimes injured or killed when cars crash into their horse
and buggies, and are assaulted and robbed because of their
Christian non-resistance.

Through the centuries Christians have been willing to
die for Jesus.

Christians have also been willing to live for Jesus.

While Christians in the Roman world experienced the
difficulties of persecution and martyrdom, Celtic Christians,
especially in Ireland had a different experience. They were
not called to die for their faith, so they created new clas-
sifications of martyrdom. They referred to persecution and
death as 'red martyrdom.' The terms 'white martyrdom' and
'green martyrdom' referred to those who left home to serve
Christ, and those who left homeland and family and served
Christ cut off from everything they knew. They recognized
that while some are called to die for Christ, some are called
to live for Christ.

Living for Christ involves a measure of self-sacrifice. Jesus very deliberately used the word slave — not a popular
word at all — to describe how we are to serve each other.
The difference is that we are doing it willingly. No one is
forcing us to be Jesus in a suffering world.

We began with a story of persecution and martyrdom at the beginning of this sermon. Now I want to talk about an example of resistance to evil of a totally different kind. There's a letter from a Christian named Kopres to his wife Serapias. During a time of persecution Kopres writes about a trip from Oxyrhynchus, Egypt, to Alexandria where he has to take care of some legal matters. When he got there he found there was a problem, but he took care of it with a little help from a friend. Here's a quotation from his letter, and a little code that's attached to the end.

> *Before all things I pray to the Lord God y'all are healthy. I want you to know that we arrived on the eleventh and it was made known to us that all newcomers were required to make a sacrifice, so I made my brother my power of attorney....99.*

Kopres noted that newcomers, people who were not residents from Alexandria, were required to make a sacrifice. At one point everyone in the empire was required to make a sacrifice, either to a pagan god or to the emperor as a god. It was a loyalty test. Christians could not perform such an act and this could lead to arrest, loss of property, and death.

Kopres got around this requirement by getting a brother (this could mean literally a brother or refer to a friend) to act as his power of attorney so he didn't have to show up in court. He didn't have to get this receipt, called a 'libelli,' which proved he'd made the sacrifice.

The letter closes with the number 99, which is a numerical code for "Amen." Christians used this code as a way of indicating their faith without broadcasting it.

Evidently Kopres could count on a non-Christian friend to make the sacrifice for him. This suggested that some non-Christians respected their Christians friends and did their best to protect them. If Kopres did not have to die for his faith he chose not to — and he continued to live for his faith.

There are similar examples from Christian Egypt of others who resisted in this way. There was a small rural congregation which, when an edict from Rome demanded all their gold and silver made it clear that their simple meetinghouse has nothing of the sort, aside from a few brass plates.

There was a Christian whose title was "Reader," which means he was the one in charge of reading scripture during worship. While giving a deposition, he claimed to be illiterate and knew nothing of any Christian books owned by the church when, during a time of persecution, all Christian books were confiscated to be burned.

Whether we die for our faith or whether we live for our faith, whether we suffer red, green, or white martyrdom, or whether we live a quiet peaceful life all our days, we are to follow the example of Jesus, serving others, living for others, and praising God.

Are you able to do this? I think so. We can all do this. That's because we're not worried about whether we're seated on the right hand or the left hand of Jesus when he returns in glory.

If we follow Jesus we do it, not for the reward, but for the regard we bear toward Jesus, and the joy we find in serving him.

We can all do this. Amen.

Not Guessing

In his book *George Lucas: A Life* author Brian Jay Jones
tells the story about how the famed filmmaker rose from ob-
scurity in the small California town of Modesto to become
the world-famous creator of the Stars Wars series. Lucas, an
indifferent high school student, became serious about pursu-
ing a career in film after surviving a devastating car crash.

His college student films attracted some attention, but
initially only a few people recognized that he had the po-
tential to become a great filmmaker. However, after fighting
budget constraints and artistic interference his film *American Graffiti* was not only a runaway hit but made millions of
dollars for the studio executives who to the very last thought
the movie was going to be a failure.

Even then he still had a hard time throughout the process
of filming *Star Wars* from executives who argued with him
about every dime, and who sat stone-faced when given the
opportunity to watch the final version of the film before its
release. Certain that it would fail, studio executives limited the number of theaters in which it would be played, and
moved the release date up to the Wednesday before the Me-
morial Day weekend hoping to cut their losses before the
summer blockbusters were released.

However on May 25, 1977, every theater in which *Star
Wars* was shown was sold out for every single performance.
Theaters began showing the film almost twenty-four hours
every day and the lines still went around the block. Then

instead of withering away after the first weekend, the Star Wars mania, including sequels, books, toys, and re-issues of reworked movies, has never stopped.

Now everyone knows what only a few people knew prior to its opening. George Lucas and Stars Wars are a real hit.

George Lucas is not Jesus and Star Wars is not the gospel, but nevertheless in the Gospel of Mark, Jesus goes unrecognized by people who should have known he is the Christ, the Messiah. People had every reason to believe in him because of his teachings, his miracles, his power over the wind and storm, and even death. While Mark makes it clear that outsiders recognized Jesus, insiders, people who knew scripture, and biblical history, those had seen Jesus walk on water, still the storm, feed the multitudes, heal the sick, and raise the dead, didn't get it.

Of course that's nothing new. Moses, through the power of God, led the people out of slavery and Egypt, and on their way to the Promised Land. These people had seen the ten plagues, the parting of the Red Sea, manna from the heavens and water from the rock. They had heard the thunder and seen the lightning and the smoke on the mountain when Moses climbed Mt. Sinai to receive the law.

Even so, they grumbled and complained, and even turned to other gods when Moses would leave them to speak with God.

Yet Rahab told the Israelite spies she hid from the vigilantes in Jericho that she knew all about how this slave nation had become a true nation thanks to the power of God.

So what happens with Jesus? His disciples ask, puzzled, who is this who calms the storm? Herod thinks this must be John the Baptist who has come back from the dead. His own disciples argue about who will be the greatest one when Jesus sits upon the throne.

But demons recognize Jesus as the Son of God Most High, which was the Gentile name for Israel's God. A centurion asks Jesus to heal his servant. A woman who was considered unclean because she had an unstoppable flow of blood knew Jesus had the power to heal her. A Syro-Phoenician woman, insulted by Jesus, refused to give up because she wanted her daughter to be cured — and now a blind man, unclean because he could not see, in an era when some assumed that sickness was a sign of sin, can see that Jesus is the Son of David.

Do you hear that? The blind man can see that Jesus is the Son of David while Jesus' followers are still blind!

This story follows the incident where Jesus caught the disciples arguing about who would be the greatest in the kingdom, and Jesus rebuked them, and taught them that the one who was the servant of all was the greatest of all. A rich man came to Jesus, described as righteous, who recognized Jesus for who he was, yet could not bear to leave behind his possessions, and walked away sad because he was not willing to leave everything behind to follow Jesus.

And now the blind man Bartimaeus sitting beside the roadside outside of Jericho recognizes not only that Jesus is the Son of David, but that Jesus has the power to be merciful to him.

This is the only time Jesus is called Son of David in the gospel of Mark, and it is an important title. God makes a promise to David that one of his descendants will always be on the throne over His people. Yet this promise seems to be broken when the Babylonians conquer Judah, destroy Jerusalem and the Temple, and take away the leaders of the people into exile.

Two generations later, when some of the people return from Babylon, there was no king, only a governor. And over the centuries during times of servitude and freedom, there is still no Son of David on the throne. Many people believed that God would restore the throne, and put a Son of David to reign over them. There were those who waited for a Suffering Servant, and some who waited for a military leader, but there was an expectancy to the time in which Jesus lived, and some wondered if he might be that Messiah they were looking for.

Jericho was a venerable and ancient city, already eight thousand years old in the Lord's day. Many consider it the oldest continually inhabited city on earth. In recent decades Herod the Great had added a hippodrome and a royal palace, but Herod also died in Jericho. For him the city was a dead end.

Jericho is also the last stop for Jesus and his apostles before he enters Jerusalem triumphantly for a week of glory, gory death, and resurrection. Soon the crowds will hail him with cries of "Hosanna! Blessed is the one who comes in the name of the Lord! Blessed is the coming kingdom of our ancestor David! Hosanna in the highest heaven (Mark 11:9-10)!"

This blind man begs money from travelers who pass him where he rests on the roadside. He is seated by the road along an important trade route, and also just outside the last stop for pilgrims on their way to the holy city.

It seems like a good spot for business. It will still be around fifteen miles, much of it uphill, for merchants, pilgrims and Jesus. They are going to Jerusalem, and perhaps it occurs to pilgrims that throwing a coin to a beggar wouldn't be the worst thing they could do before entering the Holy City. What could it hurt?

People will have the chance to drop a few coins to ease their conscience. And he is loud. Everyone's going to hear him thank you if you drop a coin, and they're going to hear him if you pass by.

Augustine, the fourth century African theologian, imagined that perhaps this beggar had fallen from a high station to this misery. According to him, the blind man "...had fallen from some position of great prosperity, and was now regarded as an object of the most notorious and the most remarkable wretchedness, because in addition to being blind he had also to sit begging." He suggested that Bartimaeus in a way stood for all fallen humanity, who are blind and should be calling out to Jesus.

At this point Bartimaeus, hearing that it is Jesus who is passing by, cries aloud, "Jesus, Son of David, have mercy on me!'

There is an echo of Psalm 6:3 in this cry. Have mercy, have pity!

Too loud. As often happens in churches, here at the roadside there are those who are more concerned with what they consider decorum or reverence. These are people who evidently have not been paying attention to the fact that Jesus has healed Gentiles, outsiders, unclean people.

There's a scene near the opening of "The Simpsons Movie" in which the Simpson family is at church (and its worth noting that as irreverent as the show is, the Simpsons are one of the few television families who regularly attend church) and Grandpa begins to speak prophetically. Speaking ecstatically, he warns everyone in the congregation that terrible things are about to occur.

In the next scene we see the Simpsons packed into their car, looking embarrassed because they've been kicked out of church, while Marge says, "What's the point of going to church every Sunday? If someone we love has a genuine religious experience we ignore it!

Do people really want to be in the presence of someone having a religious experience? Do we want people who respond emotionally and prophetically to the gospel of Jesus Christ?

In this passage from Mark a true religious experience is about to happen, but as the scripture says: "Many sternly ordered him to be quiet, but he cried out even more loudly, 'Son of David, have mercy on me!'" (10:48)

Bartimaeus would not be silent. And Jesus stopped his journey, stood still, and told the people near him to bring Bartimaeus over to him. And so the blind beggar was told: "Take heart; get up, he is calling you (10:49)."

What words! What will you say when you rise from death and you are told, "Take heart! Get up! Jesus is calling you!'

One overlooked detail of this story that when Bartimaeus springs up and goes to Jesus he throws off his cloak. More than one commentator notes that it is likely that this cloak was spread out before Bartimaeus, and that the coins thrown to him landed on the cloak. Normally he would scoop them up later, but at the moment Jesus calls him Bartimaeus rises with such enthusiasm his coins must have spilled in all directions.

Most of us don't think that there should be an economic cost to discipleship. Shouldn't following Jesus have any effect on where we work, what we wear, what we eat, or what we buy? Following Jesus should make us question if the food we eat comes at the cost of near slavery for those who pick the crops. Do we really consider whether Jesus would care if our clothes were made in a sweatshop? We think we can live in two kingdoms — the kingdom of God and the kingdom of Mammon, despite the fact Jesus said we cannot serve two masters.

What do we see here? The rich young man had walked away sadly because he wasn't ready to give away all he owned to follow Jesus. Blind Bartimaeus throws caution — and all his coins — to the wind for the chance to receive mercy from Jesus.

The wealthy man does not follow Jesus.

This blind man will.

The disciples were worried about what place they would have in the kingdom — Bartimaeus has more fundamental needs — he simply wants to see. But we see that he already sees.

What more telling gesture can we find for the joy and freedom that comes with following Jesus? Bartimaeus threw off his cloak. It could have been lost. He can't see it. He no longer has any landmarks. He is going out blindly in the dark.

He is unconcerned!

Jesus then asks Bartimaeus what he can do for him, and Bartimaeus addresses him with the Aramaic word Rabbouni. Jesus is addressed with this word for teacher only one other place in scripture — when Mary Magdalene addresses the risen Lord in the garden with that word.

Bartimaeus asks to be healed. Jesus speaks and he is healed. And as the scripture notes, "Jesus said to him, 'Go; your faith has made you well.' Immediately he regained his sight and followed him on the way (10:52)."

This is the last healing miracle in Mark's gospel. This is the last significant act in the ministry of Jesus before the fateful week in Jerusalem, and it raises questions we have to answer.

What do you see, when you see Jesus? How clearly do you see Jesus? Are you blind, though you think you see?

What are you going to choose — safety and security, or Jesus? None of us knows what Jesus will ask of us — but if Jesus asks, what will we answer?

In the Old Testament, when Hannah prayed to God in the tabernacle for a child, she prayed so loudly that the prophet Samuel thought she was drunk. Bartimaeus cries so loud that people are annoyed. Are we so worried about decorum in our church that we're not willing to let children cry aloud in happiness, or people pray with joy? Are we mistaking apathy for worshipfulness?

For that matter, are we too much of an insider to know what we've got here? Do we take Jesus for granted? Those who are hurting, those who are suffering and struggling know they need Jesus, even if they haven't heard his name yet. Will you be able to tell them if you've put Jesus into a safe box where no one gets disturbed, or asked to go the second mile?

Our church must remain accessible to those with emotion, those who are broken, those who are suffering, those who are ready to call aloud to Jesus. Our church must remain accessible to the blind, those unable to hear, those with disabilities and inabilities and different abilities.

In all of this remember the words of Jesus. Be of good cheer, rise up, he calls you. Go in peace! In wholeness. With Shalom.

Remember: Mark tells us that the blind man followed Jesus down the way.

What about you? Let us follow Jesus down the way. We have one advantage over everyone else that day. We know that way travels to the cross. But we also know that way continues past the empty tomb to the risen Jesus. Let us be of good cheer. Let us be of good hope! We serve a good Lord. Amen.

The quote from Augustine is from Harmony of the Gospels 2.65

Why the Greatest?

The late film critic Roger Ebert once said there was a great reason many critics considered "Citizen Kane" the best movie of all time. For one thing, it really is a fantastic film. Director Orson Welles combined a compelling story with a great script and creative use of pioneering techniques for filming and editing.

But he also pointed out that once you pick the greatest of anything you can stop arguing about whether something new is the greatest and focus on a new film's merits on its own terms.

He had a point. On the other hand it can be fun to argue about the greatest. In Ken Burns' ten-part documentary on baseball there is a great scene where the comic Billy Crystal simultaneously plays three kids from three different parts of New York, arguing about whose team has the best center-fielder. Is it the Giants with Willie Mays? The Dodgers with Duke Snyder? Or the Yankees' own Mickey Mantle? Each kid made a good argument but you sense that in Crystal's boyhood experience, this controversy could never be settled.

In today's gospel passage a scribe hears Jesus disputing with religious leaders, and decides to ask him the question of the day — which commandment is the greatest?

According to some experts there are 613 commandments in the first five books of the Bible, sometimes called the Torah, or the Law. Some of them are pretty familiar to all of us today, like, for instance, the Ten Commandments. Others are pretty obscure and to some extent meaningless to us. Do we really feel we're breaking God's law if we wear a shirt that blends different fabrics together, or if we eat beef stroganoff, a dish that mixes meat and dairy products?

The real question is — what is the purpose behind a law, or *the Law*? The Jewish scholar Hillel (110 BC - 10 AD) was once asked if he could recite the entire Jewish law while standing on one leg. He replied with a version of the Golden Rule: "Do not do to others what you don't want them to do to you."

He used this saying as an example of a commandment that could be considered not only the greatest, but which also encapsulated all the others. That's what the scribe wanted Jesus to do.

As it turns out, Jesus answered on his own terms. Rather than one commandment he pairs a verse from Deuteronomy with a command from Leviticus. As we shall see the two commandments chosen by Jesus get us oriented in two directions — vertically, with the relationship we share with God, and horizontally, centered in the relationship we share with each other.

The first law he quotes comes Deuteronomy 6:5, and it is known as the Shema, from the Hebrew word for "Hear!" This is the call to Israel that begins with verse 4: "Hear O Israel: the Lord our God, the Lord is one" (Deut. 6:4) The prayer, the command to "Hear!" is one that Israel was called to cherish, writing it on every blank surface and praying it daily. The reminder that the Lord our God is one, and is to be loved with heart and mind and strength is paired with the Levitical command to love one's neighbor as oneself (Lev. 19:18).

This is the first place in the Torah where the people are told to love God. They are told first to love God with all our heart. You might say that no one can be told to love someone. Love is an innermost feeling, and we can't command love. It either happens or it doesn't.

But in the Hebrew language love is not just a feeling. It's an action. Love finds expression in what you do, not what you say. If you've ever seen the wonderful musical *Fiddler on the Roof*, there's a great scene where Tevya the milkman asks his wife Golda if she loves him. They've been married twenty-five years at this point, but theirs was an arranged marriage. They never met before their wedding day. Now their children are choosing to marry for love, and not because of a parent's arrangement.

Golda responds at first by saying the question is foolish, but soon she begins to count what she's done for her husband — washing his clothes, raising their children, sharing a bed — and as she sings, "If that's not love, what is?"

And perhaps that may be the first key to how to love God, especially if things aren't going our way. We act faithfully, regardless of how we're feeling about God, and that will do for love for now.

Especially because we can't always say we love God. When we lose loved ones, or suffering a great misfortune, we may rail and rant like Job, until we see things in a larger perspective. But regardless of how we feel, we may at least demonstrate our love for God by the way we act.

So how do we love God?

First with all our heart. The word for heart in Hebrew has to do with thought and will and feeling. What are our intentions? In Jesus' day people believed in the Two Ways. There was a Good Way and a Bad Way, and we had the power to choose.

Next we love with all our soul. The word for soul, *nefesh*, is where our passions and desires, our very being, lies.

Third we love with all our strength. Literally the Hebrew words mean something like "very, very much."

Now in this passage Jesus is quoted as adding a phrase to the verse as it appears in Deuteronomy — "with all your mind." In the Greek speaking Gentile world, the mind was an important component that needed to be spoken to. The thinking person makes a rational decision for Jesus, and that is just as important as responding emotionally to the gospel's call.

The second commandment that Jesus calls the greatest extends in all directions — we are called to love our neighbor as ourselves. Because, after all, neighboring is both an unlikely and an unavoidable relationship. Many times, as apartment dwellers know, total strangers are thrown together and expected to get along.

Many of us remember Fred McFeely Rogers, an ordained Methodist minister, better known as Mister Rogers. Rather than shouting to get their attention, Mister Rogers greeted his television audience of children gently, speaking positively, encouraging, praising, and asking, musically, "Won't you be my neighbor?" The neighborhood mixed wonder, love, and security, but it was also a place where fears, and anxieties were both named and confronted.

This is where so many learned what it really meant to be a neighbor, and not just be a person who lived next door to someone. "You shall love your neighbor as yourself," is more than a commandment. It should be a reality, one that includes conflict and resolution, with God as a central player in our relationships.

Because neighbors can be annoying, exasperating, and impossible, (And sometimes we're the neighbor who's the royal pain!) one of the staples of situation comedy is the difficult neighbor. The next-door neighbor might be nosy, or rude, constantly borrowing and never returning, on the make, a gossip, even an outright thief. In TV and movies one looks to neighbors moving in with alarm, or at least suspicion? Who knows what they will bring? We laugh at the situation in a comedy, but it's no so funny when we live this reality!

Is this why most people limit this passage to one third of a verse: "You shall love your neighbor as yourself (Leviticus 19:18b)?" The larger context makes demands on us, and there are expectations required of us.

You learn you can't just make "love of neighbor" happen. You learn that you've been trained not to admit you love yourself. What does love have to do with the covenants some neighborhoods enforce with rigor?

Wouldn't a little well-deserved vengeance make us feel a whole lot better about things? And maybe that's why the command Jesus quoted from is a lot more complex — and longer — than we usually think of. However in Jesus' day when you quoted part of a verse, it was assumed you were actually quoting from the larger passage. Most of the people you spoke to in those days heard the Torah read over the course of a year in their synagogue services.

However, the context of the instruction to love one's neighbor spans two verses and requires this larger frame for an appropriate interpretation.

"You shall not hate in your heart anyone of your kin; you shall reprove your neighbor, or you will incur guilt yourself. You shall not take vengeance or bear a grudge against any of your people, but you shall love your neighbor as yourself: I am the Lord.

Put these two verses together and you get a good idea of what it means to love your neighbor. When conflict happens the one who is wrong has to confront their neighbor and confront the wrong. When the chapter in Leviticus tells us, "You shall reprove your neighbor," you have to bring things out into the open in order to solve the problem. We don't always like to do this sort of thing. We don't want conflict or confrontation in the church. But true neighboring means you have to be open about these things and face the issues squarely.

You can't solve this by wishing it would go away. If you do, you may end up doing what the first half of the verse from Leviticus warns you against — taking revenge or bearing a grudge. Don't seethe from your anger. Don't let your grudge build up.

Instead, love your neighbor, and that means recovering what you've lost with your neighbor. And what you've lost is peace.

In the first three centuries of the church Christians had to become new neighbors. They formed new families. Typically a family worked together on a shared economic enterprise. They made a product together of some sort, and gave praise to the family god. Christians could no longer worship that other god — remember the commandment — you shall have no other gods before me! Christians formed new economic families that worshiped Jesus. Since they often lived in the same household, where the business was housed, being family meant facing some of the same problems that come with neighbors.

Working toward reconciliation means recovering the relationship you had before sinning against each other. Or as it is put in the final verses of the Letter of James: "My brothers and sisters, if anyone among you wanders from the truth and is brought back by another, you should know that whoever brings back a sinner from wandering will save the sinner's soul from death and will cover a multitude of sins" (5:19-20). It is a fact that Matthew and Luke's version of this story are a little different. In Matthew the scholar asked Jesus the question about the law in an attempt to entrap him. In Luke, Jesus answered the scholar's question with a question, and it was the scholar who came up with the two laws that embody the whole law. Whereas in Mark the scholar asked a sincere question, because he was impressed by Jesus' answers to questions of controversy, and figured this guy really knew his stuff. Why not just ask Jesus the question of the day — which law is the greatest?

What are we to think since three different evangelists told this story in three different ways? I think we should remember that this question was probably asked several times first because this question was such an intriguing one, and secondly since the motivations of those who spoke was different, the response of Jesus could be different. They were certainly his terms.

The scholar's sincerity is proved by his response: "You are right, teacher; you have truly said that 'he is one, and besides him there is no other'; and 'to love him with all the heart, and with all the understanding, and with all the strength,' and 'to love one's neighbor as oneself,' —this is much more important than all whole burnt offerings and sacrifices (12:32-33)." Jesus praised the scholar — "You are not far from the kingdom of God (12:34)." And that ended the conversation.

So what are we to remember from all this?

First — Jesus answered questions on his own terms. When someone asks us a sincere question about our faith we should answer sincerely, and it wouldn't hurt if we were to think about our testimony in advance.

More to the point, we as Christians are not only to have a deep and committed relationship with God, but also with each other. Love does not go back and forth in one direction. It goes in all directions. We love God. We love our neighbor. It's not always easy. It shouldn't always be easy. But it's necessary.

And it's commanded!

Amen.

Proper 27 / Ordinary Time 32 / Pentecost 25
Mark 12:38-44

Devour And Conquer

In recent decades, archaeologists have turned their attention to ancient cooking pits and trash heaps because these reveal what ordinary people were doing a long, long time ago. Instead of assuming history is what the rich and powerful rulers were doing in ancient empires, the trash heaps and cooking pits of so-called ordinary people tell us what real life was like. They tell us about what matters to people. They give us insight into value, which may have very little with price.

Trash heaps often include bones, corn cobs, or other items that let us know what people ate and what their diet meant for their health, or lack of it. Not only that, you can measure the tooth marks on bones and figure out what people were eating, and if dogs were getting a shot at the bones as well. Knowing this can tell you if dogs were a part of their lives or not. Yes, people's trash tell a story about what life was like on a daily basis.

Let's suppose an archaeologist from the distant future was rummaging through the ruins of your home. What would give them an idea of what was valuable in your life? They may find a jewelry box, for instance, but would they know that you treasured a relatively inexpensive bauble over more expensive items, because of the associations this piece had with people or events that were special?

What if these future scientists were to discover, intact, the front of your refrigerator? Thing of what treasures they'd find? Would there be a greeting card from a friend? How about a Christmas letter detailing the events of the past year for a friend? And though expensive artwork may have hung in your home's hallway, would they realize how much you treasured the artwork of children and grandchildren affixed by magnets to your refrigerator doors?

The gift of a child's artwork can be very unassuming, and for that reason it's valuable. A child gives all they have. They pour their heart and soul into the picture they draw, so regardless of what its value might be to a major auction house or art critic, it hangs in the place of honor on your fridge.

In today's scripture passage Jesus is standing in the temple with his disciples, who seem to be transfixed by the large monetary gifts being given to the work and maintenance of the great temple in Jerusalem.

The second temple was so called to distinguish it from the temple build by Solomon that was destroyed by the Babylonians. This second temple was centuries in the making. At first when the exiles returned to Jerusalem, with a mandate to rebuild the temple given to them by Cyrus the Great, it seemed it would be a work of a few months to get the temple started, but sixteen years went by before the prophets Haggai and Zechariah lit a fire under the people and got them building again.

However it remained a work in progress for centuries until Herod the Great spent the people's wealth on finishing the project. Herod the Great was admired in the larger Roman Empire for his spectacular building projects, but those people didn't have to live under his paranoid cruelty. Though God's people loved their temple, they didn't admire any of Herod's works.

Every Jewish male was required to donate a half-shekel to the temple's coffers. Everything beyond that was a voluntary gift. Jesus was standing with his disciples near the "Trumpet Chests" that were in the women's court. The area was called the women's court because this was as far as women — Jewish women, that is — were allowed to go into the temple. Only men could go into the interior chamber. As for Gentiles, non-Jews, they were allowed in the outer courtyard, and many did so to ooh and ah at the wonderful architecture and massive columns that made this one of the wonders of the world.

According to today's scripture passage, Jesus "...sat down opposite the treasury, and watched the crowd putting money into the treasury. Many rich people put in large sums (12:21)." The Trumpet Chests were large trumpet- shaped repositories, where money could be cast for the temple's treasury. Remember, there were no checks or paper money. Cash was coin made from various metals. The coins were worth the value of the metal.

Because these were metal coins, they made a very loud sound as they clanged and clattered in the Trumpet Chests, and made another satisfying noise when they hit bottom. No doubt many could hear the coins ring and jingle, and they could distinguish what sort of coin was thrown into the Trumpet Chests by the sound of precious metals.

As Jesus watched, Mark told us, "A poor widow came and put in two small copper coins, which are worth a penny (10:42)." As a woman this widow was not required to make any monetary offering to the temple. Hers was strictly a volunteer contribution. Her tiny coins, known as leptons, made virtually no sound in comparison to the gifts of the wealthy. Those two coins, so thin you could almost see through them, made virtually no difference to the ministries of the temple from an economic sense.

Not only that, but was anyone paying attention to her besides Jesus? Possibly not, because according to the scripture he called his disciples' attention to what was happening in their midst. Jesus honored a woman whose value was not appreciated by his male disciples. They did not see her. He had to point her out. He praised her saying she had given more money than anyone else, because she gave all she had.

Scripture recognized that widows were an especially vulnerable population. In that society they did not work outside the home, so they depended upon financial support from a male relative — a spouse, a child, or another relative. Why did she give? Was it out of a sense of obligation or because she wanted to give, and wanted to be part of something larger than herself?

The average life span at that time was 25-35 years, but that did not signify how long a person lived. Many died much younger. Disease took many at a very young age. Women could be especially vulnerable — childbirth could be fatal. However, women who survived their child-bearing years might well, like today, live to an advanced age. They would outlive their husbands, their adult children, and other relatives, and require additional support.

Jesus suggested that this made her a target for unscrupulous scribes and others in position of power. Devour and conquer!

That's why the law of Moses called for widows and other vulnerable populations to receive protection.

So we read: the Lord "...who executes justice for the orphan and the widow, and who loves the strangers, providing them food and clothing (Deuteronomy 10:18)."

"You shall not deprive a resident alien or an orphan of justice; you shall not take a widow's garment in pledge (Deuteronomy 24:17)."

Exodus 22:22 says simply: "You shall not abuse any widow or orphan."

Jesus made it clear that widows, among others, need special protection. Once again, devour and conquer! That's why when the widow entered the temple Jesus had warned the people, "Beware of the scribes, who like to walk around in long robes, and to be greeted with respect in the marketplaces, and to have the best seats in the synagogues and places of honor at banquets! They devour widows' houses and for the sake of appearance say long prayers. They will receive the greater condemnation (Mark 12:38-40)."

The Scribes are an important social class. Nowadays we associate reading and writing as two sides of the same coin, but in the ancient world reading was one skill, and writing was another. Scribes could not only read, they could also write. They copied books, both sacred and secular. Scribes provided writing services to the nobility. They could keep recordings, including business accounts. They worked for the government and for private citizens.

Those who could manipulate information technology, who help control the flow of information, had great power. They demanded respect. But Jesus warned, in the imperative, saying, "Look! Don't you see what the scribes are doing?"

They wanted to look good in public, so they wore flowing robes, as Jesus put it, stoles that were associated with religious festivals. They attended the religious festivals in full regalia because it was important to them that people saw them in a great light.

But despite their wealth and power, Jesus said, they wanted more. They preyed on widows, setting them up for poor investments, where they stood to lose the homes they put up for collateral. They mismanaged estates. They took widow's houses as pledge for loans they could not pay back.

They wanted the choice seats in the synagogue. You know, some people in Colonial America, eminent families, would pay for an expensive pew so all would know how important they were compared to others who attended church.

Jesus seemed to be saying that in societies where there's a gap in incomes the strong devour the weak. Devour and conquer.

Jesus returned to the subject of widows on more than one occasion. He told a parable about an unjust judge who refused to hear a widow's court case, but in the end she wore the judge down.

Well, what are we to do? Is the warning of Jesus and the example of the widow interesting sidelights on a two-thousand-year- old economic controversy? After all, widows who found themselves without a husband, son, or anyone else, with a Jewish background can work outside the home. Nor do we throw out gifts in a metal chamber to get more bling for the buck when we toss in our gift. People write checks, use paper cash, or even electronic transfers and do so without drawing undue attention to themselves.

Also I suspect we must keep ourselves aware of the damage done by any unthinking person or church that equates a person's good standing in church with the size of the offering we make. There are always in-kind contributions for those who may not always be able to do as much as they would like with what they have.

It's a danger if we accept economic oppression as normal. It's a danger if we assume that people are poor, handicapped, or disadvantaged because somehow they deserve their condition.

When we take anecdotes as truth instead of learning that welfare queens are not the norm, and that for most poor people, being poor requires constant employment from dawn to dusk to navigate the barriers put up against them to receive what they need. Many people who are disadvantaged in ways that are not easy to detect aren't getting their food or medications. They are not getting the health care they need. They can't get to doctors and the doctors they can get to may not want to serve them.

It's too easy to criticize the spending habits of the poor, criticizing when they buy prepared food instead of uncooked food, not realizing that some people have no working stoves in their homes. Maybe their phone or their car is the nicest thing they own, because they have to rent instead of buy.

It's not enough to ooh and ah at the extraordinary generosity of the widow in this story, who gave all she had, and somehow this lets us off the hook. We should feel inspired to give more, and aspire to give all of ourselves to the work of the gospel, to the good news of Jesus Christ.

After all, some day in the distant future an archaeologist may be digging through our trash. Instead of finding the remains of our dinners, which we've stuffed down the garbage disposal or sent to the landfill, they may find our pay stubs and a copy of the record of our church giving, the original of which was sent to the IRS. They may be able to look at the bills for our phones and our television packages and make a guess as to our true priorities.

In 1895, the year of Queen Victoria's Diamond Jubilee, Rudyard Kipling wrote a poem called "Recessional." At the time the British were the high and mighty, lord of all creation, of all they could see and not see. The sun did not set on the British Empire. Against that backdrop he warned in a poem called "Recessional" that the rich and powerful (and he was referring to his own people) might, drunk with power, believe that their wealth is something they need to protect, instead of blessing those who need their protection.

One stanza in his poem says it all:

> *The tumult and the shouting dies;*
> *The captains and the kings depart.*
> *Still stands thine ancient sacrifice,*
> *A humble and a contrite heart.*
> *Lord God of Hosts be with us yet*
> *Lest we forget., Lest we Forget.*
> *(in the public domain)*

Whether we are the widow, giving all we have, or the scribes, lured by power to take even more from those who have the least, let us come before God with our offerings and with our service in humility — and joy!

Nothing can be more important than our Lord's high regard for what we do in our poverty, and nothing could be more dangerous to our souls than the Lord's contempt when we are concerned for outward appearances and what people think of us, instead of how God will judge us on that day.

Amen.

Proper 28 / Ordinary Time 33 / Pentecost 26
Mark 13:1-8

Going Into Labor

The Baldwin Hills dam was built on a steep hillside in Southern California overlooking a packed residential community. It was considered an architectural wonder, at least by its designers. It also rested squarely on an earthquake fault. The designers insisted that the fault line would not affect their structure. Nestled away on a hillside, where it would not interfere with development, it served as a storage facility for the waters that follow in the form of rain and snow melt.

Then, on December 14, 1963, a crack was discovered. The local station KTLA sent a helicopter to film the frantic repair efforts, the first time an impending disaster was broadcast live. Three hours after the crack was discovered the dam failed and the waters of the Baldwin Hills Reservoir rushed down the hillside. 277 homes were destroyed by 250 million gallons of rushing water. It was all seen live on local television!

Afterward there were recriminations and finger pointing. Who knew what and when? The dam's designer, for instance, who had also designed another dam that had failed, was adamant that his design was perfect, and that the fault lines meant nothing, when he pushed the project through. Afterward, his was a minority opinion.

What may be most important to remember, however, is that although hundreds of homes were destroyed in the merciless inundation of water, only five lives were lost. That's because an almost immediate effort to evacuate the homes was underway with the first discovery of a crack, and people not only listened, they acted — they fled their homes.

People listened.

In today's scripture passage Jesus was trying to get the people to listen! The temple in Jerusalem was by all accounts one of the great wonders of the ancient world. One can't blame the apostles for gazing in wonder at the size of the great stone blocks, and for the adornment of the temple, which makes the statement of Jesus about its utter destruction so startling. Listen! "Do you see these great buildings? Not one stone will be left here upon another; all will be thrown down."

It is little wonder that four of the disciples at least wanted to know more. Did anyone else listen? Do we listen now?

This Second Temple, as it is sometimes called, was built over the centuries to replace the one destroyed by the Babylonians. When the exiles were freed to go home to Jerusalem it was anticipated that they would rebuild the temple quickly, but sixteen years went by before any real work got underway. The temple as Jesus and his apostles saw it had been greatly expanded by Herod the Great — not that he himself did any of the heavy lifting. But Herod was greatly admired among the elite of the Empire because of his passion for construction.

One thing ancient civilizations have in common with us — many of us cannot imagine that one day our seemingly strong infrastructure will come to nothing.

In the early nineteenth century many treasures from ancient Egypt were finding their way into English museums. One well-known poet, Percy Blythe Shelley, and a journalist friend decided they ought to write a poem about a broken statue of an ancient Pharaoh. Shelley's poem, "Ozymandius," was published in a magazine called "The Examiner," on January 11, 1818:

I met a traveller from an antique land
Who said: Two vast and trunkless legs of stone
Stand in the desert. Near them, on the sand,
Half sunk, a shattered visage lies, whose frown,
And wrinkled lip, and sneer of cold command,
Tell that its sculptor well those passions read
Which yet survive, stamped on these lifeless things,
The hand that mocked them and the heart that fed:
And on the pedestal these words appear:
'My name is Ozymandias, king of kings:
Look on my works, ye Mighty, and despair!'
Nothing beside remains. Round the decay
Of that colossal wreck, boundless and bare
The lone and level sands stretch far away.
(in the public domain)

When Jesus told his followers that one day the mighty temple would be nothing but ruins, they understandably wanted to know what signs to expect so they would know such a cataclysmic thing was about to happen! Today's passage is set in the fateful week between the triumphant entry of Jesus into Jerusalem, and his bitter crucifixion. He would receive the praise of the crowds, but also their scorn. It's a week of despair, but also a week of wonder, because there is no denying that the temple of Jerusalem was a thing of wonder! Yet Jesus told his disciples a time was coming when not one stone would stand upon another.

But this kind of cataclysm is not an event that happens to someone else. It happens to us all the time.

That's why Jesus used the language of labor and childbirth to make it clear that suffering is part of what believers can expect in the face of this cataclysm. As he spoke he began to widen the scope of this prophecy from the destruction of the temple to the larger apocalypse that was to come. The destruction of the temple, which became a reality within forty years, was to be seen as simply one in a series of events, and perhaps not even the most disastrous, that would happen before God brings down the curtain on history.

Rather than make it clear what they should expect to see, Jesus, in strongly worded language, made it clear that the signs of the end could easily be mistaken for events that occur in every generation! "Beware that no one leads you astray. Many will come in my name and say, "I am he!" and they will lead many astray. When you hear of wars and rumors of wars, do not be alarmed; this must take place, but the end is still to come. For nation will rise against nation, and kingdom against kingdom; there will be earthquakes in various places; there will be famines. This is but the beginning of the birthpangs (13:5-8)."

Just the *beginning* of the birthpangs?

Who wouldn't want to know the timing of the end? There's a regular cottage industry of books and films demonstrating that the end is nigh. Oddly enough, no matter how incorrect their predictions are, people still buy their books despite the fact that every predicter has been 100% wrong. Yet every one of those writers insists they're the ones who got it 100% right!

What is the purpose of this literature? Is it meant just to frighten us? Is this the reason Jesus told his disciples to remember that everything comes to an end?

Hardly. These words are meant to comfort believers. This is why the word 'endurance' is used six times in Revelation. Hold on!

Persecution lies ahead, but it won't last forever. There's a Costa Rican proverb: *No hay mal que dure cien años ni cuerpo que los resista o aguante,* which can be translated as "There isn't any evil that lasts a century, nor will anybody have to endure anything that lasts that long either." This too shall pass. Nothing lasts forever.

People who live under the weight of injustice will hear the words of Jesus different than those who are complacent and comfortable. Many of us simply want to trade one comfortable situation for another without having to go through any trials or tribulations. But the oppressed of the earth — including those living in our times as well as those who lived in Judea two thousand years ago — the institution of God's justice and the tearing down of physical and political structures is a sign of hope.

One reason Jesus warns us against being too confident that we know when the end is coming is that the universe is full of surprises. Take the asteroid known as 2012 D4. Everyone knew it was coming, and to keep an eye out for it. Discovered in February 23 of 2012, the piece of rock was only 45 feet across, less than half the length of a football field, but it was quickly apparent that its path regularly intersected the orbit of the earth.

There was only a tiny chance it might actually hit our planet. And if it did, it was large enough to do some real damage. Even when that tiny chance turned out to be zero, scientists wanted to keep an eye on it, because in going by the earth its orbit might be changed just a smidge, increasing the odds it would hit us on its next pass.

There was a lot of anticipation when it passed within 17, 200 miles of the earth on February 15, 2013. But because astronomers were focused on this one asteroid scientists weren't looking when another asteroid actually struck the earth that day. It was an unbelievable coincidence! A smaller meteor plunged into the atmosphere and exploded over the small town of Yekaterinburg in the Chelyabinsk area of the isolated region of the Ural mountains with a blast equivalent to twenty atomic bombs the size of the one that exploded over Hiroshima, injuring over fifteen hundred people and wreaking incredible amounts of damage to standing structures!

Fortunately there were plenty of cameras pointing at the meteor's explosion over the town, not because there were astronomers looking for it, but because fake accidents and insurance fraud are so prevalent in that area most cars are equipped with recording equipment to prove falsified events never happened!

Afterward the obvious question was — how could scientists discover one meteor that would miss us, and miss the one that hit us? The answer is that it's a huge sky and there's lots of stuff up there.

Jesus might have been suggesting in this passage that there's a lot of stuff going on all the time that could be mistaken for signs of the apocalypse, so keep your eyes open or you'll miss out when the real thing happens!

Even in Jesus' time there were those who were pointing to a coming disaster. According to the historian Josephus, a Jewish writer who believed that God had ordained Rome to inherit the earth, and who wrote after the destruction of Jerusalem, "Four years before the war...one Jesus, son of Ananias...who, standing in the temple, suddenly began to cry out: "A voice from the east, a voice from the west, a voice from the four winds, a voice against Jerusalem and the Sanctuary, a voice against the bridegroom and the bride, a voice against all people....Woe to Jerusalem...Woe once more to the city and to the people and to the Sanctuary...and woe to me also." (from The Jewish War, 6.5.4 section 301, 306, 309, with a reference to Jeremiah 7:34.)

What is our response to false prophets who want us to look to the skies so we see Jesus when he returns in glory — something that is promised in scripture without any indication about when it will happen?

The proper response, according to the gospels, is to be found working! When Jesus ascended into heaven the disciples were scolded by two angels for looking into the sky instead of following their Lord's instructions. In various parables Jesus suggested that when a master went out on a trip the slaves should be found at their posts, doing their work, so they'd be found doing what they were supposed to be doing when their master returned.

The ancient Greek poet Hesiod, once wrote, "It is not work that brings shame, but not working that is shameful!" (*Works and Days,* 1.311, author's translation.)

Being alert for the return of Jesus means going about our normal tasks, whether it's farming in the fields, going to work, taking care of our homes — or serving "the least of these." The great work of the master is that we should be feeding the hungry, giving drink to the thirsty, clothing the naked, visiting the sick, and visiting those in prison – tending to these is the best way to stay alert.

Being ready does not imply a retreat from the world. C.S. Lewis, in the title essay of the book *The World's Last Night,* likened the appropriate attitude in waiting for the world's end to the anonymous First Servant in Shakespeare's play *King Lear.* The unnamed servant walks on stage when an atrocity is about to be committed by his master. Speaking barely eight lines, he tries to stop the blinding of an elderly man. That servant is killed. "That is his whole part: eight lines all told," wrote Lewis. "But if it were real life and not a play, that is the part it would be best to have acted." That is because, as Lewis put it, when the inspector arrived we were found at our post.

Take a deep breath. The world is full of surprises so we shouldn't be shocked when events catch us off guard. For something as cosmic as the return of Jesus, you'd better be alert — but keep in mind the biblical meaning of watchfulness is working for the kingdom. So remain watchful. Besides, if we're not looking we might even miss something as obvious as Christmas.

What is your post? To what have been assigned by the master? Do you imagine that it will be free from suffering? Have you heard others complain when suffering follows obeying the commands of Jesus?

Our history abounds with examples of those who followed Jesus no matter where it led. For instance, a Mennonite woman named Adriaenken of Molenaerfsgraef, wrote to her husband from prison in Dortrect, prior to her execution at the stake on March 28, 1572:

> *Hence we are of good cheer; whatever the Lord suffers to come upon us, is all for our good, for in tribulation he forgives sin; therefore his holy will be done for our profit, that is, for our salvation, which is our greatest desire, wherefore we endure everything, and are patient, according to the example of Job, prophets, the apostles, and the end of our Lord, and other martyrs after them (The Martyr's Mirror, 927).*

Earlier I mentioned how the ruins of Egypt inspired Percy Blythe Shelley to write the poem "Ozymandius." But he was speaking about ancient ruins. His friend Horace Smith wrote a poem on the same subject that appeared a month later, which no one remembers. The first eight lines were about the same subject.

> *In Egypt's sandy silence, all alone,*
> *Stands a gigantic Leg, which far off throws*
> *The only shadow that the Desert knows:—*
> *"I am great OZYMANDIAS," saith the stone,*
> *"The King of Kings; this mighty City shows*
> *"The wonders of my hand." — The City's gone —*
> *Nought but the Leg remaining to disclose*
> *The site of this forgotten Babylon.*

The final six lines, however, take a different turn, one that we might well think about:

> *We wonder,—and some Hunter may express*
> *Wonder like ours, when thro' the wilderness*
> *Where London stood, holding the Wolf in chase,*
> *He meets some fragment huge, and stops to guess*
> *What powerful but unrecorded race*
> *Once dwelt in that annihilated place.*

At that time London was the capital of a world-spanning empire greater than Rome's! Smith dared to think that his own civilization might someday be as much a collection of ruins as Egypt or Rome.

Jesus saw the ruins of Jerusalem when everyone else saw wonders. Just as the disciples assumed that the temple of Jerusalem would always stand, so we might consider that we are no more exempt from the ravages of time than anyone else. Someday our civilization may lie in ruins, because we didn't heed the words of Jesus.

And if that is so, how much more imperative is it that we be about the work of Jesus? For his kingdom will never pass away!

Amen!

Thanksgiving Day, USA
Matthew 6:25-33

Give Thanks For What?

The first Thanksgiving celebrated by the Pilgrims and Native Americans in November 1621, has been documented by every coloring page colored over by every child who ever went to school. The dinner they shared has been celebrated in every turkey drawn and decorated by every kid outlining their outstretched fingers over a piece of construction paper, cut out, glued over, crayoned up, and then framed for the wall, tacked on the bulletin board, or magneted on the fridge.

Or, bringing things up to date, photographed and posted on Facebook, tweeted, or otherwise spread by social media everywhere around the globe.

Either way, it's all part of a celebration in which we simplify the historical situation and all the players. It's unlikely that turkey looked anything like the turkey that graces out tables. They were leaner, faster, meaner, and gamier. It's not even clear if they even ate turkey.

If we talk about Pilgrims and Indians we're overlooking the fact that we're talking about a specific group of religious separatists, and a specific group of Native Americans who happened to think that an alliance with this group of Europeans might be beneficial, especially with regard to rivalries with other Native American groups.

It was complicated. Reality always is.

One thing is certain. They gave thanks to God for what they had — and that's at the heart of the holiday, however we celebrate it, and whoever we celebrate it with.

Today's passage from Matthew is a part of what we know as the Sermon on the Mount. This famous speech includes the Beatitudes, in which Jesus gave a series of statements framed as paradoxes — for instance those who seem most in need of pity are actually those who are blessed. There is a redefinition of the meaning of the law in which Jesus pointed us to the Spirit rather than the letter of the law. Jesus asked us to re-examine the way we live and look at life.

And then there's this — Jesus tolds us to worry.

Just how are we to accomplish all that? It's not like we don't have something to worry about! There are the stresses of employment. There are economic stresses. We may be taking care of our children, or we have become the parents of our parents! We may be getting much older, and dealing with the stresses that come with financial and medical complications. We may be younger and dealing with the stresses of trying to get a foothold on our future while saddled down with student debt.

The very fact that Jesus brought up the subject of anxiety tells us that people were anxious about the complications in their lives — a ruinous economy that drove many people off their ancestral land, military occupation by a distant and unfriendly foreign power, diseases that not only disabled people but drove a wedge between them and their families and villages, a much lower life span than we experience, wars, rumors of wars, and public unrest.

One way, I suppose, to rid yourself of anxiety is simply to not acknowledge just how difficult a world we live in, or they lived in two thousand years ago. One of the features of *Mad Magazine* was a character named Alfred E. Neumann, a freckled fellow with a foolish and vacant expression, who wore a button that read, "What? Me Worry?" The point of this joke is that only someone who refuses to acknowledge that there are real problems in the world can be free of worry, and conversely, the world is in such terrible shape that the only sensible reaction is to worry...a lot.

The ancient writers believed that anxiety was nothing new, but part of our lot from the beginning.

The Greek poet Hesiod wrote about a Golden Age that preceded our era, when at first "the tribes of humanity lived on earth remote and free from ills and hard toil and heavy sicknesses." However Aphrodite put into the woman Pandora "cruel longing and cares that wear out the limbs," causing her to open the jar she should not have opened, scattering all the diseases and heartaches that plague us. There was only one thing left in the jar, and that was hope!

The Greeks also invented the term "eating your heart out," referring to the way worry and anxiety consumes us.

But perhaps the Roman philosopher Seneca the Younger might help us rethink what's important and what is not. Seneca lived from 4 BC to 64 AD, and around the year 49 AD he wrote an essay called "On The Shortness of Life," about the anxiety people feel about how short life can seem. At one point he wrote: "It is not that we have a short time to live, but that we waste a lot of it. Life is long enough, and a sufficiently generous amount has been given to us for the highest achievements if it were all well invested. But when it is wasted in heedless luxury and spent on no good activity, we are forced at last by death's final constraint to realize that it has passed away before we knew it was passing."

One thing that keeps us from being thankful is that we think we need a lot more than we actually do. Seneca spoke to that when he said: "As far as I am concerned, I know that I have lost not wealth but distractions. The body's needs are few: it wants to be free from cold, to banish hunger and thirst with nourishment; if we long for anything more we are exerting ourselves to serve our vices, not our needs."

Maybe the poet Robert Lewis Stevenson (1850-1894), who did not even live 44 years, said it better, in this little poem from his book "A Child's Garden of Verses."

The world is so full of a number of things,
I'm sure we should all be as happy as kings!

We give thanks to God on Thanksgiving. The holiday as celebrated in the United States is not officially tied to any particular faith. Everyone is invited to give thanks to God. So how do people give thanks? Perhaps one model that might be helpful for us is the Thanksgiving festival we find in the Bible, Sukkoth, otherwise known as the Jewish Feast of Booths.

Once a year God's people would leave the comfort of their homes and villages and rough it in tents set up outside of town. It was not unlike a week-long family camp. Part of the reason was to remind the people how their ancestors lived in tents for forty years in the desert. They needed to be thankful for what God had done for them in the past. But they were also to be thankful for the present, as they shared the bounty of harvest time as a gift from God. The Feast of Booths (Deuteronomy 16:13-15, among other places) celebrated the conclusion of the agricultural year. Just as people shared the firstfruits at Pentecost, now they shared the final fruits of the season. This included the all-important production of wine.

After all the hard work of the harvest people were expected to rejoice as well as remember. It was certainly a time for thanksgiving, involving the whole family. As the feast is celebrated today, it involves the sights, sounds, and smells of favorite dishes that were cooked for the occasion, just like we love the smell of our favorites, turkey and stuffing, mashed potatoes and gravy, or green beans with those little crunchy onions on top.

The people also remembered that God traveled in a tent as well! The Ark of the Covenant was housed in a tent sometimes referred to as the tabernacle. When the people broke camp the Ark, representing the presence of God, went with them, and when the people pitched camp they had a visible symbol that God remained with them no matter where they went.

So what is Jesus saying to us in this passage? What wisdom did our Lord and Savior share in that Sermon on the Mount that can speak to us today?

First and foremost, Jesus gave us a change of perspective. Any Sermon on a Mount takes us up terrain taller than the landscape around us. In giving us a fresh view we also get a clue toward the real way to see things.

Jesus began by insisting the soul was greater than the needs of the body that threaten to tie us down. We certainly need food to sustain life, but we can obsess over whether we have enough, and if we do that it becomes a self-fulfilling prophecy - we'll never have enough. Then, too, clothes are necessary, but not to the point of obsession.

Jesus set out to prove his statement by calling our attention to the natural universe, in this case the birds and plants. The birds manage to get fed in most circumstances, without having all the worry and work we pour in to making sure we have enough. The same goes for the plants. Jesus pointed to the lilies of the field which manage to look more glorious than Solomon, as the Savior put it, in all his glory.

Maybe Jesus really meant Solomon in all his folly. The effort to present oneself as glorious in the eyes of others can lead to extremes of fashion that become not only absurd but burdensome.

There is reason to think Jesus was also telling us that thanks to what we call civilization we have become alienated from God's good earth, and need to look to the example of the creatures that share this earth with us so that we stress less and enjoy more.

This is not to say that we shouldn't work to raise crops or earn the money to buy food, nor does it mean we should walk around unclothed, especially in November when we celebrate Thanksgiving. One of God's judgments at our expulsion from the Garden of Eden is that we should earn our bread by the sweat of our brow. But the flip side of this is that there is a deep and abiding satisfaction in a job well done, and in the time we spend doing that job. God's grace has lifted from our shoulders the burden of the work we do when we see it in its proper perspective.

Jesus reminded us we are worth more than the very valuable birds of the air and plants of the field. Psalm 8 reminds us that we are little less than the angels. The world is here for our enjoyment. Anxiety and worry are destructive forces that take away the enjoyment from our lives and give us nothing in return for what they do to us.

In the end this passage is not strictly about the natural order, but about our attitude toward the world. The world is good, we are told in Genesis, and we're a part of that goodness. We are God's created and we are God's beloved. If we have enough, and if we work so that others have enough, we are not far from the kingdom of God.

Jesus also asked us if we can add a single hour to our lives? What does that mean? To some extent Jesus may be wrong. If we exercise, if we watch our diet, if we take the medication prescribed by our doctors, and especially if we rise above the stress and anxiety in our lives some would say that we can indeed add not only hours, but years and decades to our lifespan.

But there is an upward limit to how long a human can sojourn on this earth. Scientists may not agree about that limit, but it's there. More to the point, our quality of life is more important than the quantity. Seneca, quoted earlier, noted, "Life is long, if you know how to use it."

Returning to the book of Genesis, there comes a moment in the story of Joseph when all seemed well. Long thought dead by his brother and father, he was revealed to be Pharaoh's right hand man, the second most powerful human on the planet. In the midst of a world-wide famine Joseph held the keys to the graineries, ensuring that his father Jacob and his eleven brothers and other family members would not only survive, but prosper in Egypt.

But when Pharaoh met father Jacob, and asked him, "How many are the years of your life?" Jacob, despite the happy outcome of his life, said, "The years of my earthly sojourn are one hundred thirty; few and hard have been the years of my life. They do not compare with the years of the life of my ancestors during their long sojourn (Genesis 47:8-9)."

Few and hard — one hundred and thirty years filled with sorrows, it is true, but also great success, joys, and assurances from God.

Few and hard. It's all how you look at things.

Whatever the length of life granted to us, we can count it successful if we love each other and live to the glory of God and our Savior Jesus Christ.

Aim higher than the world. Be thankful regardless of anxiety. Work with foresight and planning, but don't live in the future at the expense of the present. Remember we can fill our barns with grain and yet be called to account at any time. How terrible to have wasted the opportunity for life and light and joy because the present is nothing to us.

Make God's kingdom your priority.

Finally despite what Jesus tells us, we can all understand why sometimes we worry about the problems of the world, our won difficulties, as well as the fragility of life. Some years it feels as if there is an empty place, even if every chair is filled, because of the loved ones who have left us for their reward in heaven. The time of Thanksgiving can include well-earned tears.

In addition to legitimate reasons, many of us worry without really knowing why. We feel pangs of anxiety and yet cannot give a name to the source of this worry. We can't always get rid of these fears just by counting our blessings, but if this is something we are bearing, let us remember at least that we are a people who can give thanks for hope. What we see is not all there is. What surrounds us, even if it alarms us instead of astounds us, is not the sum and total of God's blessings.

So let us be thankful that we have in our midst some who require our support and love, in order to be able to enjoy God's blessings. It is not enough for us to be merely content. Let us rejoice! Let us together seek God's kingdom and God's righteousness. As the scripture tells us, do this and everything else will be added unto us! We're in this together. We are saved together! We get to the finish line together.

We pass the mashed potatoes and gravy together at God's great feast! That's something worth being thankful for.

Amen.

(Want to know more about Sukkhot, or the Feast of Booths? Read chapters 7 & 8 in — "The Five Festal Scrolls" — by Robert W. Neff and Frank Ramirez)

Who Is The Prisoner? Who Is The Judge?

The Elder John Kline (1797-1864) was a doctor, a carpenter, a preacher, and an elder among the Dunkers, one of the Plain People. Kline's home was near Linville Creek, Virginia. He, like all the Dunkers, lived peaceably with his neighbors, which is not surprising since the Dunkers believed in non-resistance to violence.

For the most part his people stayed out of politics, but from their arrival in America in 1729, the group had taken an unmitigated stance against slavery. Needless to say this made them very unpopular in the Old Dominion.

After the Civil War broke out Kline refused to recognize the Mason-Dixon Line. Over his lifetime he traveled more than 100,000 miles on horseback visiting fellow Dunkers in the north as well as the south.

Earlier in the war Kline and some Dunkers and Mennonites were arrested and jailed in the local courthouse. In his diary Kline wrote:

Sunday, April 6 (1862). Rain and snow all last night, and continues on so all day. Have preaching in our captive hall. My subject is "Righteousness, Temperance, and a Judgment to Come." I aimed at comforting my brother captives and myself with the recollection that Paul was once a captive like ourselves, and that in this state of imprisonment he preached upon the text which I have selected for this day. I said:

Brethren, if any have cause to tremble, we have none. Those should tremble who seek to lay obstacles in the way of others who aim to do good and no evil. As a rule, prisoners are nervous and sometimes tremble when taken into court: but judges are proverbially calm and self-composed. Hence the old adage: "As sober as a judge." But this order is entirely reversed in the case of Paul before Felix. Here we see that Paul is calm, collected and self-possessed, and that Felix is first nervous, and soon trembles all over. In this trial it appears the judge is convicted of guilt by the prisoner himself, and the prisoner shows himself clear. But this is not the only case in which an innocent criminal has stood before a guilty judge.

(The Life of John Kline, 448-449)

Was this the only case in which an innocent criminal standing before a guilty judge? No indeed. This short passage from John, in which Jesus was on trial for his life before Pontius Pilate, the governor of Judea, also allows us to ask once again: Who is the prisoner? Who is actually free?

Jesus and Pilate verbally sparred with each other, but this was not the high school debating team. Jesus was about to die horribly. Even so, Jesus did not seem to be the prisoner. He was the king. Pilate, the representative of the emperor, who was acclaimed the son of a god and the savior of the world, seemed to be the one on trial — by religious authorities, political schemers, and even Jesus himself.

John's gospel often presents a very different picture from the other three evangelists, but all four gospels have Pilate asking the crucial question — "Are you the king of the Jews?"

Consider Pilate's confusion — he seemed to be out of his depth. He already had Barabbas in custody, a wild revolutionary, a guerrilla who sought to supplant the almighty emperor in Rome with a Messiah king. Jesus stood before him, accused by the religious authorities of seeking to making himself king, a charge of sedition which meant Pilate must try him. But is it true? Pilate needed to know if he really must upset the Passover Pilgrim crowds with an execution of someone who may be their hero, or who may just be another no one?

In the Greek language in this account the word "you" is not necessary. It is part of verb form of "to be." By using "you" John may have been making Pilate ask, almost in disbelief, "Are *you* the king of the Jews?"

"Are you someone I have to deal with?" Pilate was asking.

As often happens in the gospel of John, Jesus responded to a question with a question of his own. It is almost as if Jesus was questioning Pilate's authority. Jesus turned the tables on the governor, reversing their roles. Are you asking me this, he seemed to say, or are you someone else's pawn? Who put you up to this? Pilate revealed his contempt for the people he governed with his answer: "I'm not a Jew," Pilate answered, and he insisted that the accusation comes from the others and that was why it had come to him.

Part of the problem was that Pilate did not seem to understand the people he had been sent to govern. Earlier in his reign, according to the Jewish historian Josephua, Pilate ignored the Roman rule which forbade the display of the Emperor's face in public because in Judea it was against the commandment forbidding graven images. Pilate figured what was good enough for the rest of the empire was good enough here. But people responded by protesting, placing swords against their throats and threatening to commit a mass suicide if he did not relent.

Pilate had to relent.

Compare that to the centurion who asked Jesus to heal his slave. The local Jewish authorities spoke on the centurion's behalf, pointing out that on his own, and not because he had to, he had helped build a local synagogue in the village.

Perhaps Pilate, who may have made no effort to work with the local population nor seemed to understand their religion, may have felt he had no friends in this fight. He had to figure his way through this alone.

At the very least, one thing should have been clear to the governor — the people did not rise up in arms to protect him or to free Jesus. Other than Peter's act of cutting off the ear of a slave, one that Jesus immediately repudiated, the message should have been obvious — Jesus posed no threat to the Emperor. No political threat, anyway.

The trouble was, Jesus didn't deny his kingship — not exactly — not fully. He had just said that his kingdom was not of this world, because if that were so his followers would be fighting — the word is *agonizomai*, an athletic term that might have meant fighting but really meant contending, as an athlete would compete.

In the end, Pilate was left with a question, for which he was not equipped to receive the answer: What is truth? Perhaps he thought to himself, Okay, now we're talking philosophy. That's above my pay grade. But had Pilate taken the time to know more about Jesus, he might have heard that Jesus said, "I am the way, the truth, and the life." To follow Jesus is to accept that he is the truth, and if we wish to follow the truth, we need to keep our eyes on Jesus.

According to Raymond Brown, who wrote a long commentary on the gospel of John, we Christians may say that Jesus is Lord, or that Jesus is King, but we don't make the claim that Jesus is the King of the Jews. Yet that's why he was crucified. That's what it said on the placard above his head, on the upright of the cross. It was written in three languages, Greek, Hebrew, and Latin: "Jesus of Nazareth, King of the Jews." Whatever other accusations were made, this is the one thing that Jesus was executed for. This is the only reason Pilate really cared about.

So what does it mean to be king of the Jews? And what does it mean for us?

One of the plainest images used in the scriptures when it comes to kingship is the image of the shepherd. King David, remembered as perhaps the greatest king in the history of God's people, and certainly as the one who unified north and south into one kingdom, was a shepherd as a boy. He was considered the author of Psalm 23, a song that celebrates God's lordship through the image of the shepherd king.

The shepherd, according to the psalm, though he may be in charge of the flock, is also concerned for their welfare. He takes care of their basic needs, sees to it that they have green grass to eat and clear water to drink. Stretching the images beyond sheep into the realm of the human flock cared for by the king, we learn the ruler leads them through paths of righteousness, protects against deadly danger, prepares a mighty feast despite the presence of enemies, and creates a healthy, secure situation.

Prophets used the image of the king as shepherd, even going so far as, with Isaiah at one point says, to call the Gentile ruler Cyrus, "my shepherd," because he was sending the people back to Jerusalem from exile to rebuild the temple (Isaiah 44:28).

Jesus referred to himself on more than one occasion as the good shepherd, and at one point the gospel of John states, "I have other sheep that do not belong to this fold. I must bring them also, and they will listen to my voice. So there will be one flock, one shepherd (John 10:16)." The sheep will recognize his voice, Jesus said, because he was willing to lay down his life for him. That too is part of being the shepherd king.

The implication at least in part is that these other sheep may be part of the nations, but Pilate is evidently not part of the flock. He asked, "What is truth?" not recognizing that the Living Truth was standing before him. He did not recognize his master's voice.

When Jesus told Pilate "My kingdom is not from this world... (18:36)." He was not speaking of geographical boundaries. A kingdom's nature in both the Hebrew and Greek is very like the first definition, now listed as obsolete, in the Oxford English Dictionary: Kingly function, authority or power; sovereignty, supreme rule, the position or rank of a king, kingdom." (Oxford English Dictionary volume V, p 706.) The definition of kingdom is not about the boundaries — it's about the authority vested in the person, recognized by those who accept their rule.

Perhaps we can learn something of what it meant to be a shepherd leader in the early Christian church, after the example of Jesus. Domitian was emperor from 81 to 94 AD. He instituted a brutal persecution of Christians. At one point two of Jesus' grandnephews, the grandsons of his brother Jude, were brought before the Emperor Domitian. The church historian Eusebius recorded that Domitian feared the descendants of King David, because they were to be the source of the Messiah. Jude's grandchildren, when asked if they were descendants of King David, answered *yes*. He asked them their net worth. They replied they were worth around nine thousand denarii. A denarius was the daily wage of a day's labor. All that money was tied up in the 39 acres they owned, which they farmed themselves to raise crops for their livelihood and to pay their taxes. Eusebius says,

> *Then they showed their hands, exhibiting the hardness of their bodies and the callousness produced upon their hands by continuous toil as evidence of their own labor."*

Domitian asked them, like Pilate, about Jesus and his kingdom, and they answered,

...it was not a temporal nor an earthly kingdom, but a heavenly and angelic one, which would appear at the end of the world, when he should come in glory to judge the quick and the dead...

According to Eusebius, however, despite their relative poverty and lack of what some would recognize as a physical kingdom, the leadership and authority of these two was recognized throughout the kingdom of God.

So what about today? Is it possible to act like Jesus in a situation where your life is on the line? Is it possible that a righteous person can switch the roles of prisoner and judge? Moreover, can a person act like Jesus, turning the other cheek, loving one's enemies, doing good for those who hate you?

Probably yes.

Consider the case of Nelson Mandela (1918-2013). He was born in South Africa into the brutally unjust system of apartheid, in which people of different races were segregated by law, with blacks occupying the lowest rung in their society. He was imprisoned for 27 years, eighteen of those years in the infamous prison on Robben Island off Cape Town.

Think for a moment of all the births in your family for the past 27 years: your children, your grandchildren, or your great-grandchildren. Think of the deaths, how important each one was, and what it meant to be one family gathered together in sorrow, but also in healing and hope.

Think of the trips you took. Think of the hunts and the trophies. Think of the picnics, the family gatherings, the holidays, and the holy days. Think of the discovery of a new restaurant or the renewal of an old custom.

Can you even imagine how many phone calls you have made and received, how many letters you wrote and you got, or how many emails, texts, and tweets you have had?

Just think of ten, maybe only five, of the really high points that you wouldn't have missed for the world.

All because you are free and equal with everyone else, you can dream and make your dreams come true.

Now imagine that for the last 27 years you were in prison, much of the time in a cell eight-feet by seven-feet. Imagine that you were allowed to write only one letter a year and to receive one letter a year.

Imagine that you missed every high moment, every birth, every death, every family gathering, everything that's happened to you the last 27 years — all because you wanted to be free and equal with everyone else.

What would you feel like? What would you do when you got out? What form would your revenge take? Who would you get even with? Who would pay for all your suffering?

When Mandela got out of prison he became president, from 1994-1999. He did not take revenge on his enemies, like you and I might have. He did not call for a bloodbath and begin a reign of terror to get even with the white minority government that imprisoned him under apartheid.

He set up a commission where those who told the truth about what they'd done could receive amnesty. He worked for forgiveness and reconciliation. He met with his enemies and insisted that there had to be a way to break the cycle of violence.

That's what he practiced after 27 years of imprisonment. He practiced forgiveness.

Now some of you have really suffered. Some of you have survived truly terrible things. I'm not talking to you. Whatever journey you are walking with God through whatever pain you have endured, you have my admiration and respect.

So here's my question to the rest of us. What grudges are we holding that are so important that we cannot forgive or seek to be forgiven?

What kind of grudge are we clinging to that matches what Mandela went through? What grudge is so much greater than what this man endured, that we don't dare to forgive and seek reconciliation?

I'm always hearing people say, "I can't forgive this" or "I can never forgive that." Almost always it's for something that is really not that big of a deal.

At the beginning of this message I mentioned the Dunker elder John Kline. He stood foursquare against slavery and made no secret of it despite the fact he lived in the Shenandoah Valley of Virginia. He served everyone, at one point setting the broken leg of a Confederate soldier who was trying to escape to the north.

He respected God, but not the Mason- Dixon Line. Eventually he was murdered just a few miles from his home as he returned from the north, ambushed by Confederate guerrillas, whose identity was known to everyone in the area, and whose descendants still live near his homestead, which is now a museum to peace. In the same sermon quoted from earlier, Kline recognized that the badge of martyrdom is celebrated in eternity, when he said:

> *In the Revelation we read of a great multitude which no man could number, as standing before the throne. What a high standing they have! But by way of preparation for that honor they washed their robes and made them white in the blood of the Lamb.*
> (The Life of John Kline, 452)

Jesus is the Lamb of God who came to save us from the sin of the world. Jesus, despite the marks of scourging, the crown of thorns, and the brutality of his guards, is not the prisoner. Jesus is the king. If you acknowledge him as king, what sort of follower are you?

Are you willing to follow in his footsteps? Will you still praise him and lift his name on high when the going gets tough? Think about it. Really think about it.

What if you were on trial before Pilate? Would he recognize that you are a follower of one whose kingdom is not of this world, but whose disciples live the laws of the kingdom when they conflict with the laws of their nation? Are you willing, no matter what the cost, to stand for the kingdom of God and answer the question, "What is truth?" by pointing to the living truth named Jesus?

Amen.